Overcoming Common Problems

Other books in the same series

ARTHRITIS **Is your suffering really necessary?**
DR WILLIAM FOX

BIRTH OVER THIRTY
SHEILA KITZINGER

CALM DOWN **How to cope with frustration and anger**
DR PAUL HAUCK

DEPRESSION **Why it happens and how to overcome it**
DR PAUL HAUCK

ENJOYING MOTHERHOOD **How to have a happy pregnancy**
DR BRICE PITT

THE EPILEPSY HANDBOOK
SHELAGH MCGOVERN

FEARS AND PHOBIAS **What they are and how to overcome them**
DR TONY WHITEHEAD

FEELING HEALTHY **How to stop worrying about your health**
DR F. E. KENYON

GUILT **Why it happens and how to overcome it**
DR VERNON COLEMAN

HOW TO COPE WITH STRESS
DR PETER TYRER

HOW TO COPE WITH YOUR NERVES
DR TONY LAKE

HOW TO DO WHAT YOU WANT TO DO
DR PAUL HAUCK

HOW TO SLEEP BETTER
DR PETER TYRER

HOW TO STAND UP FOR YOURSELF
DR PAUL HAUCK

JEALOUSY **Why it happens and how to overcome it**
DR PAUL HAUCK

LONELINESS **Why it happens and how to overcome it**
DR TONY LAKE

MAKING MARRIAGE WORK
DR PAUL HAUCK

MEETING PEOPLE IS FUN **How to overcome shyness**
DR PHYLLIS SHAW

MID-LIFE CRISIS **Its cause and how to overcome it**
DR BRICE PITT

ONE PARENT FAMILIES **A practical guide to coping**
DIANA DAVENPORT

SELF-HELP FOR YOUR ARTHRITIS
EDNA PEMBLE

SUCCESSFUL SEX
DR F. E. KENYON

WHY BE AFRAID? **How to overcome your fears**
DR PAUL HAUCK

Overcoming Common Problems

HOW TO BRING UP YOUR CHILD SUCCESSFULLY

Dr Paul Hauck

SHELDON PRESS
LONDON

First published in Great Britain in 1982 by
Sheldon Press, SPCK, Marylebone Road, London NW1 4 DU

British Library Cataloguing in Publication Data

Hauck, Paul
[The rational management of children]. How to bring up your child successfully.—(Overcoming common problems)
1. Children—Management
I. Title II. How to bring up your child successfully III. Series
649′.1 HQ769

ISBN 0-85969-371-6

Printed in Great Britain at the Alden Press, Oxford

Contents

To my father and mother
who fortunately had an intuitive knowledge
of this text

Introduction

The most vital concern adults have for their children is to provide for their physical needs. Without this concern the children would die. It is amazing, however, how little it actually takes to provide these needs. Food, shelter, and clothing are the essentials of physical survival which even the poorest of families throughout history have been largely successful in providing. Today, especially, physical survival in the United States is almost a guarantee, barring accidents, and illness.

The second major concern of most adults is to raise children who know how to live in satisfaction among their associates, have happy lives, fulfill their abilities, and to be largely untroubled emotionally in childhood and adulthood. Now that their physical requirements are not taking their full energies, the parents' attentions can be turned to emotional education. However, at this task they are by and large unsuccessful. Knowledge of child management is usually fragmentary, reliance on "old-fashioned" methods is weakening, disillusionment with the "experts" is growing, and emotional disturbance of our youth remains high. Despite many of our sound religious teachings, and the wealth of material which is written on the subject of child psychology, we are faring only slightly better than we did before.

When previous child management methods were at fault, it was because they were excessively harsh and the result was many generations of guilt-ridden neurotics and psychotics. Either they turned these guilt feelings inwardly onto themselves and thereby became unsure, self-conscious, and self-hating, or they turned their guilt outwardly onto others in the form of anger, and became cruel, punishing, and excessively critical.

Today, fathers still know more about their cars, and mothers about their vacuum cleaners than they do about rearing their children. The fault is not all theirs, however. Parents have been only too willing in most instances to accept advice from professionals, and if this advice was unsound, in their ignorance they accepted it and tried it in good faith. The information for parents in the past has been either too technical, partially wrong, or totally inaccurate. Science marches forward, slowly, perhaps, but nevertheless upward, ever closer to that goal we all wish to reach: the understanding and prediction of human behavior. A sensible, workable, teachable method of correcting human behavior has evolved in the past decade which promises to satisfy what parents and other supervisors of children have been waiting for.[1] Though it has been highly successful with adults and children, literature in this field has not yet dealt with the latter. This is the first attempt to my knowledge to bring the principles of Rational-Emotive Psychotherapy (R-ET) to the adult world to assist it in its task of raising sound and undisturbed children. It is teachable to the average intelligent parent, can be very brief, and appeals solely to reason. Now the adult does not need to be a skilled psychotherapist, or a dream analyst, or have studied abnormal behavior for four graduate years to satisfy his second most important concern for his children; sound emotional development.

The Rational-Emotive therapeutic school of emotional correction can often assist a grownup purely through his reading of the principles of R-ET. Difficult problems, of course, will

1. Ellis, A., "Reason and Emotion in Psychotherapy," New York: Lyle Stuart 1962.

require the individual attention of a skilled counselor but a thorough familiarization of these principles and the errors commonly committed by adults can help them help themselves. In the following pages will be found a concise and hopefully clear discussion of the new thinking in child management as practiced by this psychologist in his own practice with a diversity of problems which have been corrected through the application of pure reason.

My faith in this method stems largely from years of dissatisfaction with the other standard systems of child treatment. Psychotherapy based on Freud's principles (the analytic model), play therapy, and client-centered counseling, have all proven only moderately successful. After searching for better and briefer methods, I am convinced of the vast superiority of R-ET over other techniques.

CHAPTER I

New Thoughts on Emotional Disturbance

Many theories have appeared which have attempted to explain the causes of emotional disturbances. These can be grouped into roughly three categories: The Environmental, the Affective, and the Cognitive.

The Environmental Theory

This view regards mental illness as the result of stressful events. It holds that these happenings in and of themselves, are the direct cause of emotional tensions. The layman does not hesitate to assert, for example, that a child cried because he was teased. He believes literally that the teasing was a *direct* cause of the crying. In the same vein the layman believes that his neighbor was *made* depressed because he lost his job, or that his coming home late actually infuriated his wife.

The average person finds this a very common-sense view and he accepts this theory almost exclusively. Such remarks as: "She made me mad," "That was a funny movie and made me laugh," give clear evidence of this belief that the events in our lives have a direct, one-to-one relationship with our emotional feelings.

No distinction is made in the layman's mind between being influenced by environmental events of a physical nature and environmental events of a psychological nature. If a sharp knife can cause a physical pain, they reason, then sharp, cutting words can cause a psychological (emotional) pain.

This theory leaves totally unexplained why some events bring on tears one day but not the next, or why one person is perfectly calm over an unfortunate event while another person, exposed to exactly the same frustration, has an anxiety attack.

As we shall come to see this theory makes good sense, but only to a point. As popular as it might be, it is nevertheless inadequate to explain in any comprehensive fashion the phenomena of emotional upheaval.

According to this view, relief from emotional distress usually involves an attack on the problem "causing" the tension. As long as the problem remains, there is generally little that can be done about the accompanying feelings. Since the former is thought to be the cause of the latter it follows logically that the removal of the problem would always remove the distress. Such is often the case, of course, but it does not necessarily remove strong emotional reactions once they have started. If a child has once been seriously frightened because he nearly drowned and soon developed a phobia for large bodies of water, we could probably give him much relief by having him live in the desert. There is a chance, however, that he could develop a new fear, or that his fear would return the moment he was placed beside a lake again.

Whether it be someone's anger, short funds, or demotion in school, those holding to the environmental view of disturbance rely practically completely on the removal of the problem to reduce the distress. The child will feel better only when his friend is no longer angry with him. The father will stop worrying only when he can pay his debts. And the adolescent girl will stop feeling inferior only when she can make up the lost grade.

In short, emotional pain is created *by* our problems, therefore relief is impossible unless the problems are removed.

The Affective Theories

The most widely held professional views of mental disorder are those which attempt to find the unconscious emotional experiences a troubled child has undergone and then to bring these forgotten and dreaded memories up to the conscious level of awareness so that they can be seen in a more realistic light. Until these fears or guilt feelings are made conscious, the child supposedly lives with this corrosive material in his subconscious mind where it is out of sight but still very active and alive. He may be jealous of and hate his father whom he fears will harm him for these evil thoughts, but will refuse to recognize the true nature of these feelings. The child may feel so guilty over this hatred that he longs to be punished for his wickedness. As he is not consciously aware of his hatred he will not realize that the many senseless accidents he seems to have are his means of punishing himself.

According to this view it is not the environment, such as the father who is creating the disturbance, but rather the boy's unconscious feelings (or affections as they are technically called). Relief is achieved only when the *feelings* are understood and relived again with a person who will not punish the boy for his harmful wishes.

A kind psychotherapist would encourage the child to talk about his private feelings or to enact them in play therapy. Under his encouragement the boy would allow more and more of his raw and forbidden emotions to show until they are completely uncovered and the boy is face to face with his unconscious wishes. The therapist would be careful to accept and love the child even after this terrible knowledge were laid bare.

When the child sees that he will not be harmed for having these drives he relaxes and thus gains emotional relief.

This, of course, is a very brief and incomplete description of the affective therapies. Thousands of books have been written about these theories, the most famous of which is the psychoanalytic model founded by Sigmund Freud. Client-centered couseling founded by Carl Rogers, a psychologist, is another model of an affective theory of emotional disturbance. We need not go into these or other models at this time. For our purposes it is sufficient to understand that all such theories attempt to make the subject aware of the unconscious feelings which lie behind the symptoms. Problems as such are largely ignored. It is believed they will fade out of the picture once the unconscious is made conscious and the child is shown how he was creating his own problems without knowing it.

The Cognitive Theories

Presently there is only one major cognitive theory worthy of discussion, Rational-Emotive Psychotherapy founded by Albert Ellis (1962). According to this theory (R-ET for short) mental suffering does not come directly from our problems or the unconscious feelings we have over them but rather from the conscious or unconscious irrational and false notions we have about them. To regain emotional equilibrium we need only identify the false idea or ideas held by the child; then, through the rigid use of logic he is shown and convinced how irrational these ideas truly are; and finally he is encouraged to behave differently in the light of this new knowledge. This and this alone is all that is required to calm an emotional disturbance. It matters not whether the child was demoted, or hated his father. Any distress he may feel concerning such matters comes solely from his incorrect notions about them. If they are realized to be incorrect, the disturbance vanishes. Though it would help to remove the problems, R-ET demonstrates that peace of mind is possible whether these problems are solved or not since it is not the problem but our thoughts about them which make us tense. Shakespeare said, "It is our opinions of things which torment us, not the things themselves."

Let us look at an example. An adolescent becomes rebellious because he feels his mother is giving him a greater share of the work than his brother is getting. The Environmental View would settle for just that as an explanation of the boy's disturbance. The Affective Theory would attempt to show the boy that he is not really jealous of his brother but rather of his father over whom he has been jealous since babyhood. The attempt would be made to get him primarily over his father-jealousy for then his problem with his brother would practically dissolve of its own.

The Rational-Emotive View is concerned with getting him to see what he believes, to find the false ideas among these beliefs, to convince himself of their falseness, and then to practice not making himself angry again.

In this instance the boy is probably telling himself: 1) my brother is favored by my mother; 2) I wish my mother wouldn't do more for him than for me; 3) it's unfair of her to favor him, 4) since I don't like what she's doing she shouldn't do it. On close examination, we can see the last thought as being the neurotic one since he cannot prove to us it is correct. He will, of course, answer that a good mother does not play favorites. To which we can answer that she hardly *has* to be a good mother. He may then reply that she's *supposed* to treat her sons alike and not play favorites. This we counter with, "Why shouldn't she?" She would have to be perfect never to show some favoritism. Obviously, she cannot be above error, so she can and will make this mistake. Further, just because he does not *want* her to like his brother more than him, why does that mean she *cannot* if she jolly well does? He would obviously be wiser to recognize that she has every right in the world to be unfair if she chooses and that if he wants her to change toward him, he may have to change his approach.

Emotional correction would involve three steps. First, we must show the boy which beliefs are wrong, namely that it is a catastrophe because he is not getting his way, and that his mother's unfair treatment of him is actually and literally disturbing him. Secondly, we would reason with him until he saw how incorrect both of these assumptions were. With examples and logic we would argue that not being favored is hardly a tragedy although it is an irritation. We would further demonstrate through reason that his *reaction* to his mother rather than her behavior is really causing his disturbance since he is not being physically abused. Thirdly, he would be advised to be doubly sweet and cooperative. For example, he could pick a bouquet of flowers for his mother every day. He could do his chores and then some even before she asks him. If these do not work he still need not be upset and angry since his past experience has shown him amply that this makes matters all the worse. Instead he can learn to accept things as they are and make the most of them. There is never any good reason for becoming emotionally upset over anything we can do little or nothing about. This is an imperfect world and to demand that it be perfect is foolish.

These neurotic reactions can best be described if we regard them like superstitions. A superstition is a false belief. The idea that spilled salt can cause us bad luck, or that a broken mirror or a black cat crossing our path will doom us for some time to come has been taught to all of us during our childhood. While we believed them as children we became worried and fearful when these events happened.

Most of us do not believe them any longer, however. Why is this? Simply because we thought hard and long about them one fine day in our youth and decided with the help of logical reasoning and analysis that these beliefs were pure hogwash.

The moment we showed ourselves that these beliefs were truly nonsense, spilled salt, broken mirrors, and black cats failed thereafter to disturb us.

These are normal superstitions. They are not the only superstitions we are taught, however. There are at least eleven neurotic superstitions we have been taught from childhood through our parents, teachers, friends and neighbors, TV, books, and movies. Dr. Albert Ellis has made a great contribution to the field of psychology by showing us what these eleven irrational ideas are and how they can cause emotional disturbance. In brief review they are:

1. The idea that it is a dire necessity for an adult human to be loved or approved of by virtually every significant other person in his community. No matter how hard we try we cannot get everyone to like us, and as long as we can still get enough cooperation from others to satisfy the essentials for physical survival, we truly do not *need* others' approval although it is perfectly fine to *want* it.

2. The idea that one should be thoroughly competent, adequate, and achieving in all possible respects if one is to consider oneself worthwhile. This represents a demand for perfection, something which is seldom attained and most often downright impossible. We get better and better at things only through making numerous errors and then correcting the errors with further trials.

3. The idea that certain people are bad, wicked, or villainous and that they should be severely blamed and punished for their villainy. People cannot help being people, that is, imperfect mortals who will often behave less than perfectly simply because they are mentally defective, ignorant and unskilled, or emotionally disturbed. Punitively punishing or blaming people for their sorry behavior has more often the effect of increasing their misconduct. Our penal systems and the endless examples of brutality from history give clear evidence for this.

4. The idea that it is awful and catastrophic when things are

not the way one would very much like them to be. Getting terribly upset about the injustices of the world does little or nothing toward curing these ills. In fact, the more one focuses and worries over life's tragedies, the more unpleasant one makes one's life; hardly a remedy to be recommended.

5. The idea that human unhappiness is externally caused and that people have little or no ability to control their sorrows and disturbances. In the final analysis, the external environment can only cause us physical pain, never emotional pain. The latter comes from within ourselves when we believe things which are illogical and we act upon them.

6. The idea that if something is or may be dangerous or fearsome, one should be terribly concerned about it and should keep dwelling on the possibility of its occurring. Chronic worrying seldom achieves the results calm deliberation and careful study do. If the danger is averted it is despite the over-concern, not because of it. In fact, excessive, neurotic worry often incapacitates the person to the point where the feared event is not avoided, but actually brought about.

7. The idea that it is easier to avoid than to face certain life difficulties and self-responsibilities. Doing the easy thing first and settling for immediate relief or pleasure is practically never as rewarding as delaying one's pleasures for the fruits that come through hard work. The proverb, "A stitch in time saves nine" expresses this idea nicely.

8. The idea that one should be dependent on others and needs someone stronger than oneself on whom to rely. A truly sound feeling of self-confidence comes not from what others do for us but what we can do for them and for ourselves. Mastery of the skills we wish to conquer comes only when we decide to do our tasks rather than have others do them for us.

9. The idea that one's past history is an all important determiner of one's present behavior and that because something once strongly affected one's life, it should indefinitely have a

similar effect. If a person will seriously question the irrational beliefs he is presently guiding his life by, he can change his behavior no matter how long it had influenced him in the past. Man *can* learn, even how to unlearn a strong influence from childhood.

10. The idea that one should become quite upset over other peoples' problems and disturbances. We can do pitifully little in controlling the emotions and behavior of others, but we can do a great deal about controlling our own. Though we may want and can do something about another human's behavior, there is still no need for us to be upset over his problems. Only a sensible attack through action can change his problem, not the degree to which we become upset.

11. The idea that there is invariably a right, precise, and perfect solution to human problems and that it is catastrophic if this perfect solution is not found. The world can simply not be so thoroughly known that perfect solutions to our problems are possible. One is better off thinking of several possible solutions and then trying each one if it seems the present plan is unsatisfactory.

These then are the neurotic superstitions we are all raised with. Practically all emotional disturbances can be traced to one or more of them. In helping a child over his emotional state an adult should help the child look for the idea or ideas he holds, locate the irrational ones, and demonstrate to him through reasoning how that idea is truly irrational. This can sometimes be done with one attempt; it sometimes needs many attempts. The adult should make every effort to teach his child to think clearly rather than crookedly, regardless of how often the issue comes up. After mother or father have challenged and questioned these beliefs often enough for the child, most often he begins to learn how to do it himself. When he accomplishes this he is well on his way to a more stable, emotionally satisfying existence. Then, when his emotions are under control, the child can be shown what to do to relieve his problem, a thing he will have far more sucess with at this point because he will not get any interference from fears, jealousies, moods of despair, anger, and so on. The deck will be cleared so to speak; the proper task of calmly solving his problems (if they can be solved) will proceed, and he will also learn not to be disturbed over his problems if he cannot solve them for the time being, or forever for that matter.

This is the new view, new, because reason has been seriously mistrusted as a method by which to maintain our mental balance. Yet it is a gift from the ancient Greek philosophers who, along with a few outstanding thinkers throughout history, have been reminding mankind for hundreds of years that our disturbing emotions come only from our own disordered thinking.

The objection will be made that very young children cannot be approached through reason. It is true that a lower limit exists beyond which reason is futile. I personally, however, have reasoned with five-year-olds with gratifying results. When logic is beyond them a change in the frustration itself (as the Environmental Theory advocates) will have to be made. A two-year-old cannot easily be talked out of a fear of a large dog. Removal of the dog, or the child, will soon bring peace.

12. The idea that it is vitally important to our existence what other people do, and that we should make great efforts to change them in the direction we would like them to be.

People find it quite difficult to grasp the point that forcing others to behave sanely (and this is especially true of children) frequently makes them rebel against that sane advice. In the final analysis people will behave as they *choose* to behave unless we have such complete domination over their lives that we can actually force them to do as we command. A prison guard and a warden have this control over prisoners. But a parent, despite his insistence that he has this control over his children, is as wrong as he can be. Children are not prisoners and will exert their wills against dominating parents in so many devious ways that mother and father are often made completely exasperated as they attempt to engage in a neurotic power struggle with a child.

The twelve irrational ideas listed above were offered by Albert Ellis, Ph.D. the creator of rational-emotive psychotheraphy. A thirteenth irrational idea has occured to me:

13. The idea that beliefs held by respected authorities or society *must* be correct and should not be questioned.

This makes little sense because no one is perfect, and what we honor today is often cast aside tomorrow. No one, regardless of how much he was respected in his day, was totally free of stupid thinking, free of urging ridiculous ideas upon others, or free of being just plain asinine. The same applies to institutions, whether they be governments, universities, or churches. Each has had its share of propagating plain nonsense. The healthy person is not awed by reputation or title but attempts to think out clearly what is being offered and to do so solely on the value of the belief, not on who holds it.

CHAPTER II

Erroneous Beliefs of Child Management

Most of us have our pet notions as to how children should be raised. The majority of these notions are false and injurious to children. To do the best possible job of being parents we must get rid of these false beliefs and substitute new, more sensible ones. We have found the following errors to be rather widespread. Let us see what they are and why they are erroneous.

Error Number One

CHILDREN MUST NOT QUESTION OR DISAGREE WITH THEIR SUPERIORS

We have all been taught to respect adults, and in particular to "honor thy father and thy mother." And this is as it should be. It merely attempts to make the child aware of the superior wisdom and experience an adult may have, due to the many lessons he has already learned in his lifetime. However, to discourage our children from questioning and disagreeing with us is an inefficient method of child management for the following reasons:

1. It places the adult in the ridiculous position of playing God. We can never be right at all times, and some of the disagreement we get from our children may well be because they are right and we are wrong. The mother or father, however, who insists always on total agreement from his or her children is making the claim that if he or she says or believes something, it must be accepted and never challenged simply because it was the grownup who made the statement. Interestingly enough, they would never demand this sort of neurotic compliance from adults. But if these same beliefs are questioned by one's children this is viewed as disrespect.

These people suffer from a confusion between disapproval for their beliefs and disapproval of themselves as persons. They believe that an arguing child necessarily thinks less of *them* because he thinks little of their beliefs. This is a fallacy which all perfectionistic and conceited people must come to understand is not so. Since we are not perfect we will often be in error. This does not detract from our own worthwhileness, however, since that is the way we were made: imperfect. Such adults feel uncomfortable and ashamed of this imperfection and judge themselves *by* their successes and failures. Therefore, a child who disputes his parents' wisdom is thought by them to show little respect for *them* when they are only showing disapproval of their *thinking*.

The calm, mature, and self-assured parent accepts his less than God-like wisdom and does not feel threatened and under fire. To him honor is a thing to work for, not demand. Disputes over his opinion are not taken in a personal way. These adults will receive honor when they learn how to honor the rights of others.

2. Silence does not mean agreement. Merely because a child has been silenced and forced to comply to his superior's direc-

tions is no proof that he actually agrees with them. The difference of opinion may exist as strongly as ever (and probably stronger than before) merely because the child was forced to agree outwardly. In such instances, however, no real change of mind has occurred. He has probably agreed to the dictatorial assertions of his mother and father only on the surface while in his heart he holds fast to his private opinion. This is an empty victory for the adult since it closes all avenues for really changing the child's mind. Nothing constructive has been accomplished. Two parties started out with differing views, both of them expressed. In the end two parties still have differing views, but only one of them is given voice.

3. It does not help the child think for himself. If we want to prepare our children for an adulthood in which they are to navigate a course by themselves we must encourage them in the skills of thinking correctly. If the adult does all the decision-making, the child will become dependent upon him. Then he will increasingly doubt his own decisions. Once this happens the adult will be even more put out with the child because he shows no leadership, independence, and sureness of himself.

Correct thinking can only be taught by hearing what the child has to say, regardless of what or whom it disagrees with. Only when his views are in the open can they be examined and corrected. Once they go underground they can become fixed and often extreme.

4. It asks the child to be untruthful. In all likelihood, a child's disagreement stems from his sincere belief that he is right. He may be grossly in error of course, but until this can be shown to him, his view, for him, is correct. Therefore, when the conceited grownup demands total agreement he is really telling the child to lie to himself. An adult need only imagine how he would feel if someone forced him to agree to a viewpoint he actually opposed.

Rather than force our wills upon their thinking, let us recognize their right to disagree, as well as their right to be wrong. If we cannot change their viewpoints, let it rest. If we are right they will more than likely see it someday. If we constantly use our authority and make them agree, they will comply outwardly only.

5. It can create guilt. If a child is accused of breaking one of God's commandments each time he finds fault with his parents' thinking he can hardly help but develop intense feelings of being evil, sinful, and wicked. This stems from the confusion between disapproval and honor. They are not the same. It is perfectly possible for a child to honor his parents and to disagree or quarrel with them over issues at the same time. This method often works at making the children superficially more agreeable but the price for this agreement is immense and not worth it. Prolonged guilt feelings almost always lead to the child's hating himself, and this in turn is a direct route to emotional disturbance.

6. It denies them the most essential tool for control of the emotions: the ability to reason. As we shall see in what follows, reason is the weapon that slays the dragon of negative emotions. In every case I shall cite, teaching the child to reason and see how he was thinking illogically was the primary cause for improvement, whether the symptoms were bed-wetting or poor grades. To achieve this correction in his faulty thinking the child is encouraged to reason, to ask endless questions about his most treasured beliefs, to debate with his superior and with himself, to challenge everything until he knows for good reason why he holds his beliefs. This is itself a brief description of what counseling is all about.

Is it small wonder that our pet notions (adults must not be questioned, and an inquisitive mind is regarded as rude and disrespectful) cause emotional disturbance? These work in precisely the opposite direction as does the work of therapy. The one discourages open debate, intellectual challenge, and reliance on reason; the other encourages them. It is safe to say the adult who adheres to this notion is planting the seeds for future emotional pain.

Error Number Two

A CHILD AND HIS BEHAVIOR ARE THE SAME

One of the most common and serious errors we commit on our children is to judge them as good or bad people, by their actions. That is to say a bright student is thought to be a better person than a dull one; a moral girl is regarded as being a better human being than a wayward girl; and a skilled child is judged as being a better child than an unskilled one. In each of these cases the person involved is judged either good or bad depending upon whether or not the behavior is good or bad. In short, a clear demarcation is not being made between behavior and the person who commits the behavior. As a result, both are denounced despite the sensible religious teachings that we should deplore the sin but *always* love the sinner.

This kind of thinking makes sense only if it is possible for humans *never* to misbehave or act stupidly. It fails to accept human beings for just what they are: human. To be human means precisely that: to act in less than God-like ways. If we could act with perfect wisdom and morality in every instance, we no doubt would do so. We do not act like superhumans, however, because we are not superhuman. Therefore, we must expect less than perfect behavior from creatures that can do no better. We must expect illegitimate births, murder, war, laziness, and emotional disturbance in the same way we must expect people to have heart attacks, cancer, and diabetes.

We do not judge a person as being horrible when he has a horrible disease. We clearly separate his disease from him in our thinking. Why then should we judge a boy as being bad because he commits a bad act such as setting fire to a house? He must have done it for a good reason or he would not have done it at all, just as there is always a good reason for having a disease. "But what 'good' reason," you ask, "could a boy have for burning a house?" There are at least three good reasons which account for any and all objectionable behavior:

1. The child has low intelligence. If such a boy sets fire to a house it would be his mental inability to understand the potential danger of matches which would account for this criminal act rather than his supposed "criminal tendencies." His act in this instance could have been a truly tragic one, but should he be blamed for doing something he had not the intelligence to understand? He is accountable for the act since it was he and no one else who committed it. But, he is not worthless, bad, or wicked because he did an irresponsible thing. We should instead expect people with low intelligence to commit such senseless acts.

2. The child was ignorant or unskilled. If an intelligent child sets fire to a house and did not want to, he must have done it by accident. Perhaps he dumped his father's ash tray in a can with gasoline-soaked rags. Does this make him a bad boy, or only an uninformed boy? Surely we can agree that if he had known the rags were in the can, he would not have done it. He has therefore a very good reason for starting the fire: total ignorance.

3. The child is emotionally disturbed. As we are coming to see, mental illness which is not caused by physical means (brain damage, old age, toxic drugs, etc.) is really caused by illogical thinking. These emotional disturbances *are* false beliefs, or irrational thoughts people have, and this can occur to bright and dull alike; intelligence is no guarantee against sloppy, inaccurate thinking.

If people do not think clearly, or have never been taught to do so, we should not be surprised if they behave in senseless, childish, neurotic ways. Thus, a child who made himself angry because his parents would not let him attend the movies might set the house on fire out of spite and revenge. This would not be due, however, to his inborn wickedness but rather to his honest, but totally false beliefs that a) his parents have no right to frustrate him, b) everything he wants he must have, c) his parents are wicked and should be punished, and d) burning down the house will teach them never to frustrate him again.

Each of these beliefs is irrational but the child does not think so. He is doing what he thinks is absolutely right. How then can he be bad? Obviously he is not bad but rather misinformed, and, therefore, upset.

*All misbehaviors are clearly the product of stupidity, ignorance, or disturbance. Prevent mental retardation; inform, educate, and train the ignorant; and teach rational thinking to the disturbed. Then the only problems man will have to contend with will be those of Nature, Chance, and Time.

Error Number Three

CHILDREN CAN UPSET THEIR SUPERIORS

This error is without doubt one of the most serious made by adults and must be corrected before good child management can proceed. To do this we must understand the difference between three sets of terms: physical vs. psychological attack, frustration vs. emotional disturbance, and desires vs. needs.

Physical vs. Psychological Attack

Any harm done to the body by an outside force, or by denying the body its essentials such as food, liquid, air, and warmth can be called a physical attack. Such assaults can be committed against us by others, by the environment, or by ourselves. The pain from such attacks is real and caused by the person or thing which committed the assault. To make this more clear, let us say a person steps on a nail and feels pain in his foot. If we call the nail A and the pain C, it *is* logical to conclude that the nail caused the pain, or that A caused C.

A psychological attack on the other hand is always committed only by people against other people. Furthermore, environment cannot pain us psychologically, only physically. Therefore, we distinguish two kinds of pain, physical and emotional. If a child says, "I hate you, mother," this is an aggressive statement which is frustrating to the parent because she is hearing something she does not want to hear, and the mother may become quite upset over these words. Let us call the child's words A and the mother's reactions to these words C. Are we still correct in concluding that the upset was caused by the words? Can we say A caused C as we did in the case of a physical attack? Practically everyone would say "yes." But this is totally incorrect. If we but think this over carefully we will realize that mother was not hurt by these words since the words cannot cut her skin like a knife, or break a bone like a car accident might, or deny her of food, air, or warmth. Only a physical attack can do that.

Yet she is upset. If it was not her child's nasty remark which upset her what was it? It was the thoughts she told herself after hearing her child's comment. Let us call these attitudes, opinions, or silent sentences B. It is B therefore, and not A, which caused her to be upset at C. We feel according to what we think. If we tell ourselves angry sentences at point B we will feel angry at point C. If we say sad sentences at B we will feel sad, depressed, and listless in our bodies (point C).

Frustrations vs. Emotional Disturbances

Whenever we are upset we are not correct in saying "you upset me," or "that upset me." No, what really happened is that someone or something *frustrated* us and we have now upset ourselves *over* the frustration. The adult, to become calm, must first ask himself "What did I say to myself just before I became upset? I must have convinced myself of something that is foolish or untrue. Let me find what that sentence or belief is and then I'll examine it and try to convince myself that belief is truly false." When these false beliefs are thoroughly challenged, emotional disturbances dissolve. Notice, we have not said the frustration (point A) disappears, only the disturbance (point C) *over* the frustration is reduced. Ridding oneself of the frustration (if it can be done at the time) is an entirely separate task and can be accomplished much more easily after the guardian is calm again. (More of this under Error Number Ten.)

Suppose the mother had said to herself, "The poor child is upset. I wonder how I can calm her? In the meantime I needn't take her seriously since her saying I'm hateful doesn't make me so. That's her opinion because I didn't let her go to the movies. Anyway, children will be children so I must expect this sort of behavior. That doesn't mean I have to let it go. On the contrary, because I dislike this kind of talk I'll have to penalize her so she doesn't act like this the next time I frustrate her." By having such calm, unblaming thoughts at B we can readily see how the mother will soon be undisturbed at C.

The following diagram will show this more clearly:

Physical Attack

A	————————	C
Nail	causes	Pain

Phychological Attack

A	———————— B	————————————————	C
Child's Words	Mother's Thinking About A	causes	Emotional Disturbance

This brings us to a startling conclusion; no one can ever upset us, we always upset ourselves. This is true whether we are talking about minor frustrations, such as having it rain on the day we planned a picnic, to a death in the family. Unless the pain has been physically inflicted by someone or something directly on to our bodies, the pain is caused by our own incorrect thinking, nothing more.

Desires vs. Needs

A third reason for Error Number Three (children can upset their superiors) has to do with the confusion adults have over desires and needs. The adult who *wants, wishes,* or *prefers,* certain behavior from children and is then frustrated will only experience a disappointment. He will certainly not be seriously upset since he has not made the issue overly important. All of us have been disappointed over literally thousands of desires without serious consequences whether it was to be rich or famous.

When we convince ourselves, however, that we *need* riches or fame, that it is *necessary* to have well-behaved children, then we have changed these harmless and healthy wishes into neurotic demands. A demand which is not satisfied will create intense feelings of anger. It will not have been the disappointing behavior of the child which will have created our disturbance but rather our unreasonable *demand* that they do as we *wish* them to do.

Error Number Four

PUNISHMENT, GUILT, AND BLAME ARE EFFECTIVE METHODS OF CHILD MANAGEMENT

For centuries parents have punished their children in righteous anger, let them think they were bad for acting badly and if they could also make the child feel guilt over his behavior so much the better. In truth, these techniques have often worked in subduing children but at too great a price. Child management to be sane and helpful must satisfy three standards:

1. The discipline must not become a new crime, for who then is really misbehaving? To cut off the hand of a thief may cure him of stealing but is sure to create more problems for him.

2. Undesirable behavior must become more desirable in

some other way. It does not profit the child or the adult if a thumb-sucker is cured of this habit only to start wetting the bed.

3. The child must not only change in his outward behavior, but in his inward thinking as well. If a criminal leaves jail with the same set of attitudes he went in with, his confinement has accomplished little. A child who is forced to change but who does not agree with the reason for the change will comply only in the company of adults and do as he really thinks as soon as he is on his own.

Harsh physical punishment, blame, and guilt satisfy none of these three criteria. In fact, they lead *to* the criticism mentioned above. Let us look at each in turn.

Physical punishment and blame are aimed more at revenge than correction. They are, therefore, almost always carried out while the adult is angry. At least five unhealthy effects develop from disciplining in anger. 1) Abusive words such as "stupid," "slob," etc., which usually accompany a scolding or spanking, eventually take their toll on the child. He believes eventually, he is precisely what he is being called. Since it sounds like his parents or teachers loathe him, he soon loathes himself. 2) The next logical effect is a loss of confidence in himself. "How can I trust myself to succeed if I am worthless? It's hopeless," is the child's attitude. The clearest sign of this attitude is his feeling of inferiority. Perhaps the back slumps, the head hangs, eye-to-eye contact is avoided. The boy or girl looks and acts like a whipped puppy with its tail between its legs. 3) It is difficult even for mature people to continue trying to do a task they are failing at. Yet, only by trying, failing, studying the failure and trying again is improvement made. How much harder it must be for children! People who have experienced some success in this learning process know that practice and hard work will usually lead to some degree of mastery.

*The child who has been scolded, punished, and corrected

with anger is so fearful of being treated this way in the future, he soon learns the safer course of action is no action. He is afraid to try again. Yet repetition is the very act necessary for improvement since most tasks need practice. Fearing practice, he becomes more and more inept at more and more tasks. Eventually he can justly regard himself as an inadequate person, a failure at everything he tries.

4) It is quite natural that people want to be perfect. However, after they have failed and been angrily punished for their failure, they make success an all or nothing thing. From this comes the subtle but sick change between desiring perfection for oneself, and demanding perfection. Once this mental attitude is adopted the subject is likely to be tense at each task since he now worries whether or not it will be perfect. Since perfection is seldom the lot of us humans, it is inevitable that much emotional disruption will result from the pursuit of this impossible goal.

5) Even if the child recognizes the adults have been correct about his behavior, he tends to develop resentment and hatred for these punishers when they correct him with anger. The issue of whether they are right or wrong is soon lost sight of and a similar attitude of revenge develops in him which he sees so clearly in his superiors.

Rather than punish with physical force it is much better to discipline by showing the child the logical results of his misbehavior.[1] If he will not do his chores, let us not give him an allowance. If he will not make his bed, forbid him to sleep in it. Let us act rather than scold or sermonize. These frustrations can be employed with deliberation, calm, and reason. The child has lots of time to think over his misbehavior and because he is not in physical pain, or being yelled at, his mind can concentrate on what he might do to avoid such unpleasant penalties in the future.

---

1. Dreikurs, R., and Grey, L., Logical Consequences: A New Approach to Discipline, New York: Hawthorn Books, 1968.

Guilt in particular has been regarded as absolutely essential to good conduct. Take away guilt, it is felt, and moral life would collapse. There is no proof of this whatever. Millions of crimes and immoral acts are committed by people who have experienced intense guilt over their past transgressions, but who went on breaking their moral codes. If guilt is so efficient a method to control behavior why do we have so much misbehavior?

The sad truth is that guilt confuses the child's thinking so much that he does not know how to avoid it. To avoid stealing and the penalties which go with it, the child must have the presence of mind to think calmly about how inefficient stealing is as a way of getting what he wants, and he must instead think out better methods, such as working, saving his money, making a trade, etc. His mind must be free to solve his problem. If it is ridden with guilt and feelings of worthlessness we see at once that he is not likely to do a good job at solving his problem because he is not thinking about his problems at all. Instead he is thinking of how bad and how hopeless he must be. The problem of why and how he could overcome stealing is being ignored while he gets depressed and cries himself to sleep. Of course, guilt sometimes works, but at what price! The guardian who makes her child feel guilty for dirtying up the house by telling him how he is driving her to the grave will no doubt succeed in getting him to be more orderly. Again, however, we are likely to develop another undesirable habit in its place since he must feel wicked and "bad," after hearing her tell him so time after time. Wicked people are expected to do wicked things. The boy, convinced he falls in this category, will behave as he believes he is.

In summary, physical punishment (except as a last resort), blame, and guilt tend to create emotional disturbances and misconduct rather than reduce them. A system of carefully applied penalties, applied without guilt or blame, is much more likely to bring on the desired behavior because the focus is on the *problem*, not the value of the *child*.

Error Number Five

CHILDREN LEARN MORE FROM WHAT THEIR SUPERIORS SAY THAN FROM WHAT THEY DO

"Do as I say, not as I do" is familiar advice given many children by adults who know only too well they themselves cannot often follow their own good advice. Yet so strong is the belief that lectures and advice are enough to train children, we ignore the obvious fact that we are always repeating ourselves. Why? Because more than advice is needed. We must be prepared to do what we advise.

If a parent shows through behavior that he seldom becomes angry over frustrations, he is giving evidence that what he says works. If it is possible for him it is possible for the child.

A child who is told he can control his temper at all times but sees his parents quarreling most of the time cannot take their statements seriously. He naturally wonders why they don't follow their advice if it is so good.

Verbal description can only go so far in teaching a skill. Imagine a painter or mechanic trying to describe only with words how to paint a landscape or adjust a carburetor. As a picture is worth a thousand words, so also is a demonstration. Parents who themselves save money can teach this by example so much more easily than parents who are careless with money.

Obviously more than merely setting an example is involved. If mother who is a perfect housekeeper nags at her daughter to keep a clean house, the resentment over the nagging may be so intense the girl may well have a sloppy house of her own someday despite the good example set by her mother.

If the adult has been reasonable with the child but a cherished lesson has not been learned, it can usually be assumed that the adult was not practicing as he was preaching. Our actions are so much a part of us we easily become unaware of them. A perfectly well-meaning person may scold her child for procrastination yet not realize this is one of her biggest faults which the child is copying. This, in fact, is one good way to become aware of our own unconscious habits: observe our children. More than we realize it they are imitating us.

Error Number Six

PRAISE SPOILS A CHILD

Most normal adults welcome praise and recognition for their good works. In fact, much of our effort as adults is to gain recognition, respect, and perhaps even praise from our friends and associates. Praise is regarded positively, not shunned. We glory in it and seek it everywhere. Strange to say, some of these same people who have no fear of receiving praise for themselves, actually believe that praise would be bad for their children. If the child performs well, it was expected and does not call for special attention. "He's only doing what he should be doing" is their attitude.

Actually, adults are often reluctant to praise children because they would feel embarrassed to do so. In most cases they themselves have had parents who always took good work for granted and seldom gave special notice to it. They are, therefore, unaccustomed to praising and feel strange about it when a situation calls for it.

Several important facts about praise should be remembered:

1. Praise the act, not the child. This has reference to Error Number Two (a child and his behavior are the same). Just as a child is not bad for behaving badly, so he is not good for behaving well. The child is always a worthwhile person and his behavior for the moment merely reflects his intelligence, knowledge, skill, or emotional control. Therefore, it is logical to praise a boy's skill at playing basketball, but not sensible to conclude that he is a better person than those who do not play as well

as he. If we believe he becomes a better person as he improves his game, we must also conclude he is a worse person as his game declines; hardly a true statement.

2. Praise acts like a reward and strengthens the behavior. Complimenting a child for cleaning up his room will encourage him to do so again the following day. This system of rewarding desirable behavior is well known to animal trainers. With their pockets filled with bits of fish they teach seals to balance balls, bark, or dance, merely by feeding them each time they please their trainer.

3. A child who is having *only* his behavior corrected or praised cannot help feeling good about himself. He, his personality, and his worthwhileness never come under question no matter what his behavior is like, and for this reason he need feel no offense or have his head turned by praise, since it is his *behavior* not *he* which is being considered.

4. In the final analysis it is what we allow children to do, not what we tell them, which spoils them. Lack of control, not excessive or foolish praise, leads to spoiling. Often the two go together, but this is coincidental in that we tend to allow behavior we would also praise.

5. If a parent is going to err on the question of praise, he is doing less harm if he over-praises than under-praises. A child will be less troubled going through life with his nose in the air than scraping the ground. As he matures, he can more easily accept himself as less perfect than he imagined whereas it is more difficult to see himself as better than he thought.

Praise, if properly applied in a sincere fashion to the child's behavior can be the finest food for his personality growth. If confined to the behavior, he cannot be fed too much. The dozens of "Thank you," "Nicely done," "Awfully considerate of you," "How sweet of you," "My you look good," "You certainly tried hard," etc. throughout the day are helpful and need never be spared.

Error Number Seven

CHILDREN MUST NOT BE FRUSTRATED

It is said we cannot escape death and taxes. This piece of wisdom should be amended to include "and a multitude of frustrations." Life is a series of problems, even for the most fortunate of us, and hardly a day goes by that we do not experience some frustration. For this reason a great many parents, out of love and kindness for their children, work hard to protect them against practically all of life's hard knocks on the belief that life will only too soon force its unpleasantness upon them. This is indeed a selfless and noble desire, but regrettably too often carried to an extreme. The truth of the matter is that much frustration, since it is an inevitable part of life, should not be denied them. The thinking parent concerns himself more with the task of helping his children learn to remove frustrations by themselves if possible, or to live with them if this is temporarily or permanently impossible. These are important goals for the following reasons:

1. The protective parent who takes over his child's problem may well make that childhood troublefree but is sure to make his adulthood infinitely more frustrating. Unless mother and father live forever, this child is not likely to be treated by other adults in the same indulgent way his parents treated him. When this happens, the indulged and protected child will be called upon to deny his own desires for a time, to permit others to have their way, to delay in his own satisfactions, and perhaps never have his desires filled. To do this will require practice and skill: one is not born with frustration tolerance, one is trained at it. To reach adulthood without this skill is like being a non-swimmer on the ocean in a boat which has just been deserted by two life guards.

2. Life takes on color and flavor from the problems and challenges it offers. The over-protected child cannot help but

get bored by this tame and unexciting life. This boredom can be a greater frustration and source of unhappiness than many of the misfortunes his folks helped him avoid. In short, the goal of a life with few displeasures is impossible.

3. True happiness comes with the ability to a) avoid unnecessary frustration, b) remove or minimize problems after they arise, and c) live calmly with those that cannot be removed for the present or forever. These three aspects can well serve as a definition of maturity.

The considerate adult, therefore, tries to be fair to each child, and tries to avoid favoritism. Since this is not always possible, he need not apologize for some of his mistakes, for these mistakes can be good for the child's growth. Let him make the most of our blunders. Let him endure unfairness. We, too, have a right to our imperfections. It is not harmful to our child (unless done to excess) to be reprimanded for something he did not do, or not to be allowed a movie show merely because we may not have a good reason for his not going. If the authority is sometimes accused of playing favorites, so be it. Most adults do so at one time or another and being only human this can never be totally avoided. Rather than the parent feeling guilt over this unfairness, let the child bear it. Merely because he wants perfect parents is no reason why he must have them.

This earth is not a paradise or a heaven. It is not managed by superhuman, flawless people. Let us, therefore accept it with its limitations, always ready to improve it but never childishly insist it must be better. And let us teach this to our children.

Error Number Eight

HEAVY PENALTIES WORK BEST IF APPLIED FIRST

A common belief held by many authorities is that punishments should be severe enough to correct the misconduct in question plus all other forms of misconduct. They trust in the notion that "one for good measure" will spare them further problems. Where a simple denial of a privilege such as not watching his favorite TV show for one night might be enough, for example, the child is also fined half his allowance, and kept in the house after school for a week.

At first glance this method might seem sensible since the child can hardly fail to get the message, yet nevertheless it has serious drawbacks.

1. A grossly unfair and excessive penalty is likely to breed resentment in the child who may then turn around and defy his parents in overt, passive, or subconscious ways. For example, he may now argue with his little brother instead of his parents, or go "underground" and frustrate them by bringing home poor grades.

This is admittedly senseless behavior on the part of the child but once his righteous indignation rises he is more content to give his parents a hard time than to look out for his own welfare. To him, the price of getting even is never too great, even though he cut off his nose to spite his face.

2. A wise general does not waste his heaviest artillery on destroying one jeep. He has a sense of what his weapons can do and in which circumstances they ought to be employed. Should he use all his heavy ammunition against a small danger, he then has nothing but rifle fire against a group of tanks.

The parent likewise, who takes a child's allowance away for a month, makes him do dishes alone for a week, and forbids him to attend school functions for the rest of the term is hard put for sensible penalties in the future. The child often does not heed these penalties since he reasons that his parents are not worth obeying, for things cannot get much worse anyway.

3. When these punishments with the added measure do work, alas, they tend to work too well. Not only does the child fear committing the original infraction again, but he is wary of his harmless acts as well. He may now fear not only talking

up to his parents, but also to his playmates. The lesson has been over-learned; it has become over-generalized.

Fear spreads to other situations remarkably easily. A frightening experience in the dark while at camp can cause a fear strong enough to persist at home, in the streets, or the movies. Darkness itself is now feared by the child, not a specific darkness such as a dark night on a country road which caused him to fall into a deep ditch and break his leg.

This fact has been demonstrated numerous times in the laboratory, and every psychologist is familiar with it in his many contacts with his troubled clients. A child who is frightened by a loud gong while eating near a rabbit does not only learn to fear rabbits, but all soft and furry objects as well, such as cotton, or Santa Claus masks.

The discipline must fit the deed, not exceed it. It should be applied gradually, getting more intense by degrees. If a child skips his daily half hour of piano practice, start by doubling the period for a week. When the week is over, return to the half-hour period and study the success or failure of the penalty.

Should another practice period be skipped in the next week or two, repeat the same penalty. It might be wise to do this a number of times since in all likelihood the lesson will soon be learned if it is given calmly and consistently.

If it does not work the parent will have to be somewhat creative and figure out a logical consequence for not practicing. He might calmly admit to the child that perhaps it was a mistake to take lessons in the first place and that they can be discontinued if the child is prepared to devote that time for playing the piano over to other work that must still be done. Johnny has a choice, in other words. He must now decide whether to practice his piano for an hour a day and permit his mother to do all manner of chores, or to give up the piano and take those chores off her hands. If he chooses to give her mother an hour a day at such things as washing windows, mowing the lawn, cleaning out the toilet and vacuuming the carpets, then mother should agree to let him do it as long as it is understood that he can change his mind later. In any case, the child chooses and peace remains in the family even though one of mother's aspirations may never be fulfilled.

If the parent is not satisfied to make such an agreement with the child because she feels it is very important to learn the piano, she can still often win the day if she will gradually increase her penalties and while doing so be very sweet about it. The less harsh and scolding she is the less likely it is that the child will think of rebelling. The use of gradually increasing penalties however, always runs the risk of creating a minor revolution. When this happens serious feelings are created which can tear a relationship apart for years. Rather than push a child to the point where he resorts to obnoxiousness it is better to back off, and let him make his mistakes. More of this will be explained in the chapter on discipline.

Error Number Nine

A CHILD MUST EARN HIS PARENTS' LOVE

Parents intuitively feel that reward tends to strengthen desirable behavior and punishment to weaken undesirable behavior. Therefore, they reason that love, a great reward, should be given as a reward for good conduct and withheld as punishment for misconduct. This notion is deceptively simple and misleading for it almost invariably leads to unexpected complications.

1. Just as we would not take away his books to punish him for a poor report card, so we must not withhold our love because he misbehaves. For the grades cannot improve without

books available for study, and behavior cannot improve when we demonstrate through holding back our love that the child is unworthy of it.

We might just as justifiably decide that our children also had to earn their bread and butter. After all, they had no choice in the matter of being born and for that reason we recognize our responsibilities as parents to give them what they need to grow, both physically and mentally. Food, shelter and clothing are required for physical well-being, and love is required (for chilren at least) for emotional well-being.

2. To use love as a payment for good conduct is terribly hard on the learning process. It is literally a feast or famine proposition. The child is either a king or a beggar and his mind cannot relax enough to control his behavior if every action is going to head to such extremes. He focuses instead on *what* is going to happen to him, not *how* he might solve his problems at the moment. In other words he becomes distracted from the task at hand. Try to imagine how much you as an adult could learn about your job if you knew that one mistake would get you fired. Then you have some idea of why a child cannot profit from his experience either when his entire security is in the balance for each and every action.

To do his best a child must never worry over being loved and thought worthwhile. With this security in the background his energies of concentration and analysis are free to study and evaluate his actions. When he fails he will be calm though regretful and look back on his performance to see how it might be improved.

Error Number Ten

CHILDREN SHOULD BE CALMED FIRST, ADULTS SECOND

As parents we are continually being frustrated by our children. This is a fact of life which will never change. All behavior between people is frustrating at one time or another. We can only hope to minimize these frustrations, never eliminate them totally. Can we conclude, therefore, that happiness depends upon how much frustration one has to face? That is, will Billy, because he has at least three significant problems or "crosses to bear" such as a drunken father, poverty, and an unpleasant job at the garage after school, be more unhappy than Tommy whose parents are both in good health, are well-to-do, and who has a car of his own to cruise around in after school? Perhaps many people would automatically say Tommy must be happier than Billy. And perhaps they would be right. However, they could just as likely be wrong since happiness depends not on our frustrations or deprivations (short of physical pain) but on our attitudes over our deprivations. Billy, therefore, could well be the happier of the two boys although he is the more frustrated. Although Tommy has "everything" he may whine about not having a newer car, or not enough spending money, or time to enjoy himself away from homework. In short, he may feel quite miserable.

This example merely serves to show that a frustration and emotional disturbance are different. To repeat, our children frustrate us (give us problems) but they do not disturb us or make us unhappy.

In 99% of the families this is not understood. What they believe is the following:

1. We upset children by frustrating them.
2. They upset us after they become disturbed.
3. To restore peace and harmony, the child's emotions must first be calmed.
4. Then the parents' disturbance will ease off.

This may seem like simplicity and logic itself, but it is inaccurate and only works sporadically. We have just seen that a frustration does not need to lead to a disturbance. This applies to children as well as parents. Therefore, their problems or disturbances, which are our frustrations, cannot in turn upset us unless we allow them to do so.

Let us regard our children's frustrating behavior as Problem Number One, and our emotional reactions to Problem One as Problem Number Two. Thus, Robert, who is bringing home poor grades is frustrating us since he can do much better but won't. This is Problem One. We could calmly think over this problem and decide to make Robert study harder, take away some of his privileges, or get him a tutor. If these measures do not work we can calmly think up other solutions, and these failing perhaps accept the boy as a poor student.

Most parents, however, do not take such a calm approach. When faced with a frustrating problem, they usually upset themselves: Problem Number Two. Instead of having one difficulty to deal with, they now have two; the frustrating child *and* their uncomfortable emotional reactions to him. Often this second problem becomes far more annoying than the first. The child who won't eat his cereal is hardly the problem to the parent as the parent is to himself after he spoils his own breakfast by yelling and getting angry. If this were not inefficient enough, the parent usually commits another error at this point; while he himself is still upset (Problem Number Two) he attempts to deal with the child (Problem Number One). This can often be a serious mix-up in priorities. Before problems outside of us can be solved we must first solve our own. The disturbed parent cannot do a good job of managing his or her children while still disturbed. Unless the adult is physically or emotionally in shape, his efforts at dealing with the outside problems will always be inferior to what they otherwise might be.

A mechanic cannot fix an engine (Problem One) while his hands are cut and bandaged (Problem Two). He must first let his hands heal before he can do efficient work on the car. Should he work on Problem One before he removes Problem Two, he is likely to do a poor job on the engine and create more problems. A housewife who wants to vacuum and dust her house (Problem One) but who is weak from a fever (Problem Two) will probably break things or scratch furniture, etc. To do a good job she must first consider herself and regain her strength. Then she can sensibly turn to her household chores. The same holds true for the management of children. A mother who has made herself very angry over her daughter's disobedience and does not try *first* to calm herself, will only cause her daughter more resentment by treating her in a blaming, critical way. If the child has a good reason for her behavior the angry mother will not have the presence of mind to listen to it. Furthermore, whether or not the child has a good reason, the mother will more than likely do all the wrong things to correct her child. She may become far too harsh for what the misconduct calls for. She may say things she does not mean, the child may become more disturbed, and in turn the parent will become increasingly angry, and so on.

Good child management proceeds along these lines:

1. We frustrate our children, who then, because of their immaturity, upset themselves.

2. We accept this as Problem One, to be worked on and solved, not as a reason for us to create Problem Two (self-disturbance).

3. Having remained calm and limiting our problems just to one (outside of ourselves) we devote our attention to the child and apply all our knowledge to helping them calm down also and *then* teach them to remove, minimize, or avoid future frustrations.

CHAPTER III

Patterns of Kindness and Firmness

We have seen in some detail the common errors made with child management. These and other errors can be grouped under a simplified scheme which coincides with actual observations of families and permits us to think of management as four kinds of patterns: 1)unkind and firm, 2) kind and not firm, 3) unkind and not firm, and 4) kind and firm. We shall see what the characteristic results are in shaping children depending upon which of these paterns predominates in a family.

Unkind and Firm

This combination produces most of the neurotic signs we meet with daily. The worriers, the tense and anxious, the depressed and suicidal, have all been raised with unkindness and firmness. Children having specific fears such as of the dark, injury, failure, dogs, in short, phobia-like reactions have been widely and intensively exposed to much blame and much domination. Parents who run their families according to this neurotic scheme set hard and fast rules from which they do not bend and they set up a master-servant relationship between themselves and their children. Soon the child regards the world in superiority versus inferiority terms with him at the inferior end and most everyone else at the superior end.

His supervisors blame him for his weaknesses (Error Number Two—A Child and His Behavior Are the Same) but do not allow any questioning of their authority (Error Number One—Children Should Not Question Or Disagree With Their Superiors). Any wrong-doing is handled consistently, quickly, but it is also accompanied by unnecesary harshness, by an attack on the personality of the child, and by an effort to make him feel guilt (Error Number Four—Punishment, Guilt and Blame Are Effective Methods of Child Management). Having constant blame heaped upon him, the child cannot avoid developing a poor image of himself which naturally leads to more poor behavior. Soon he has proof himself that what his supervisors think of him is true. Inevitably this self-blame will produce depression, either mild or severe, over even the slightest of human failings.

This approach: unkind, blaming, critical, but firm was almost traditional a few generations ago. It produced millions of responsible and hard-working adults who were guilt-ridden and unhappy. It is still practiced widely today although it seems to be lessening, especially under the impact of the "permissive" schools of child psychology.

Among the other common errors committed by these parents are: Error Number Six—Praise Spoils a Child; Error Number Eight—Heavy Penalties Work Best if Applied First; and Error Number Nine—A Child Must Earn His Parents' Love.

If we mentally stack the amount of blame these children get on the left and the praise on the right, these two piles are always unevenly balanced, which causes these families to have problems in which the children are submissive, overly obedient, and fearful. They may fluctuate between depression (self-blame), anxiety (expectation of blame), or defensiveness (blame of others). Only when the praise is increased greatly over the blame so that the weight of the two piles has shifted completely do we bring these children back to a more happy disposition.

The one redeeming feature of these families is their ability to remain firm. Their children are seldom spoiled because work and responsibility have been demanded of them. They fall short of good management on two accounts however, they blame, criticize, and do not love their children when they misbehave, and they fail to praise them when they do. Of the three steps in good child management—1) never blame, 2) be kind and firm, 3) praise—supervisors whose pattern is unkind but firm must improve their skills on the first and third points; never finding fault with the child, only with his behavior, and showing him love and praise at all times regardless of his conduct.

Kind and Not Firm

Adults, over the past two decades, have been blamed so consistently for being unkind and too firm with their children, that they have now gone too far in the opposite direction to correct their former ways. Being kind but not firm creates worse problems for society though it slightly improves the life of the child. In the past we raised responsible, hard-working children but they were also self-blamers and thus, suffered greatly from guilt and feelings of worthlessness. Today, we tend to see many more children who shirk responsibility, who make many demands, who feel the world owes them a living, and who are not the workers the children of former generations were. But they feel less depression, guilt, or shame. Instead, their complaints are boredom, lack of fulfillment in life, a realization that their undisciplined talents remain underdeveloped. They sense their helplessness but lack the self-confidence to do anything about it, except make further demands upon their caretakes.

This, of course, is a concentrated picture which applies to

many of the children today who have emotional problems and whose parents realize their children are not growing up to be the independent and happy adults they thought they were raising. Actually, this pattern (and this includes the other three as well) has always been present during all ages. During these times, however, we are seeing an emphasis on it rather than on the former pattern which was so prevalent years ago.

This method of child management tends to rear the spoiled brats, the weak and dependent, and the emotionally infantile. What else can one expect if a child is treated very kindly by letting him have his way, making few demands, and placing no limits on him? This might work somewhat if it were balanced with firmness. Without that balance, however, kindness becomes a dangerous thing. The most common error these parents commit is Error Number Seven: Children Must Not Be Frustrated. Not seeing the value of making a child work for his goals, or the genuine value of not giving him everything we could give him, the child does not learn to do without. He never masters the art of living with frustration or unfairness and simply does not learn to tolerate them.

One reason these children get their way so often is that they protest loudly when not pleased and the adults permit themselves to become upset over these scenes. This is Error Number Three: Children Can Upset Their Supervisors. Rather than become more stern with them and thereby overpower the child's tantrum, these parents end the tantrum by gviing in to it, so great is their desire to rid themselves of the disturbance they created themselves, but which they believe was created by the children. Had they remained calm in response to the child's behavior and merely penalized it appropriately they would find no need to end the struggle so quickly since they would not have an inner disturbance to get rid of.

Another reason for their inefficiency is Error Number Five: Children Learn More From What Adults Say Than What They Do. These adults sabotage the little firmness they do employ by contradicting themselves between their words and actions. They may believe they are quite firm because they show great concern over the child's grades and tell him to study each night, or that he should not play out of doors on the eve of test, but in their behavior they let the child know that they will not stop him. Actions speak louder than words. What sounds like authority, when put to the test by most children sooner or later, often turns out to be nothing but the roaring of parental winds.

When these parents do decide to get tough they usually wait until they are so fed up with the child's behavior that they become extreme in their punishment or completely surprise the child with their great outbursts of anger. The heaviest penalties are applied first rather than built up to gradually (Error Number Eight) and these penalties strike the child as unfair for the misconduct in question. The parent often sees this as being true also and he feels guilty after getting severe. Seeing his parent having regrets, the child does not learn the intended lesson. He thinks his dad, because he apologized about the way he disciplined, also feels he was wrong in that he disciplined at all.

A child who has not been taught to tolerate frustration because he was treated too kindly by his parents will run into numerous problems as an adult. He may want to speed or break a rule without realizing that the law will not be as forgiving as his parents. Only after numerous arrests and reprimands from social authorities do these individuals learn the hard fact that the law and most other people will not tolerate what was allowed at home.

In their marriages and on their jobs, these spoiled darlings also expect others to make all the adjustments to their whims. When they are disappointed they become angry, resentful, quarrelsome, and even indignant. The other person's viewpoint is seldom considered. Only theirs has merit. The potential difficulties between marital partner or fellow empolyees is obvious.

Rather than be kind and not firm, these parents would do

well to be kind but firm. Specifically, they must take a stand and mean it, both in word and in deed. Then they must expect the child to protest loudly, and even flare up in a tantrum. This second piece of misbehavior usually frightens these parents who are surprised and guilty over this much disturbance because the second misconduct is sometimes worse than the first. Unless they remain firm with each action and the *protests* to the penalties of these actions they weaken their position of authority and eventually allow the children to win the power struggle.

Children raised according to this pattern of errors are often the least understood since they can be rational, adjusted, and charming when they are getting their way. Under frustration they rampage and lose all dignity. By consensus they are regarded as emotional infantiles, but often not as disturbed people. This is an error because they are as emotionally disturbed as other people who come to the attention of the psychologist, but in different ways.

Unkind and Not Firm

This is a particularly devastating combination, very much like the previous one we just looked at, but even more serious. At least the last pattern had the saving grace of showing love and acceptance even though it was not handled wisely. This pattern lacks even the warmth of that mistake.

The unkindness is usually shown by believing the child is deliberately trying to behave poorly and that he could easily improve if he had a mind to. The fact that he does not often change for the better after he has been scolded, criticized, and denounced is further proof to the parents of the child's basic wickedness and meanness (Error Number Two—A Child and His Behavior are the Same). In all likelihood his good behavior is taken for granted and little is done to reward him when he has pleased his parents (Error Number Six—Praise Spoils a Child). The child is now in a bind. He is rejected if he misbehaves but not particularly accepted if he doesn't. He is almost as damned if he does as he is if he doesn't. To guess that he will be confused is an understatement. Certainly he will be confused, but in addition, very frustrated (since he never seems to win either way) and very angry and resentful. At this point is decided whether the child will turn these hostile feelings inwardly or turn them loose on those close to him or on society in general. If the parents are firm we have the pattern which produces all forms of neuroticism or psychosis (unkind and firm). If the parents are not firm, the child can very likely develop into a delinquent (Error Number Seven—Children Must Not Be Frustrated).

One common reason the child behaves disorderly is to bring out this very firmness from his parents. He regards their indifference as a sign of rejection and then attempts to prove to himself that if he behaves badly enough they *will* care for him and make him mind. When all he gets is further criticism for his misdeeds but no meaningful action to make him behave he is driven on to test them further to see how great their indifference is. All the while, the confused parents become more indifferent and helpless refusing eventually to give their child love since he hardly has been deserving of it (Error Number Nine—A Child Must Earn His Parents' Love). They fail to realize that the correction of undesirable behavior requires more than words and reasoning. If these fail to work then misconduct must be penalized. Continued vengeful punishment, scoldings and guilt will only let him believe he is as bad as he feared he must be to be treated with so much contempt and indifference (Error Number Four—Punishment, Guilt and Blame are Effective Methods of Child Management).

Much of the anti-social behavior we see today is a product of this combination of errors in child management. Excessive drinking, petty thievery, gang warfare, and other forms of vandalism, etc. can often be traced back to a family pattern of unkindness coupled with lack of firmness. If not corrected during the adolescent stage other forms of anti-social behavior are often practiced as adults.

Of the three elements recommended to handle each behavior—1) never blame, 2) be kind but firm, 3) praise—these parents are weak on all counts. The unkind attitude can be checked by calmly discussing the objectionable behavior and the kind of behavior which is expected instead. Then the penalties can be applied firmly and with consideration for the extent of the offense; and finally the child can be accepted all the while and his other acceptable acts and deeds praised even while the undesirable acts are being criticized and penalized.

Kind and Firm

Of the four patterns this is the most desirable. Practiced in its finest and most skilled form, these parents do some of the following quite consistently.

1. They do not hesitate to talk over with their children the conduct they find objectionable. In doing so, however, they make it a point to focus always on the act itself, never on the child or his personality. The child is told, "Son, I don't like the fresh way you talk to your brothers and sisters," not "I don't like you because you talk fresh." Regardless of whether the child tracked mud across the floor, broke a window, or was arrested by the police, these parents do not delude themselves about the seriousness of the problem but they still reserve all their attention to correcting the problem, not to making the child feel awful, repentent, and blameworthy. Even while they are telling him how displeased they are with his behavior, and how they regret placing stern penalties upon him to correct his behavior, they never attack him. Instead, they regard the problem as a normal part of life, an inescapable reality which must be dealt with, and which can probably be overcome in the majority of cases if they think of the misconduct as a problem which needs a solution, rather than as a

deliberate insult from the child, committed only to vex his parents. They believe in the inherent goodness and worth of each human being who can more easily show this goodness if it is taken for granted. Any problems, frustrations, or irritations which are caused by their children are viewed as normal results from either low intelligence, insufficient knowledge or skill, or emotional disturbance. Rather than attempt to find fault with the child they try to correct his lack of knowledge, or train him in the skill, or teach him to think calmly. If this cannot be accomplished, their goal is to accept as much as is possible to gain.

2. Secondly, they realize that life is a series of problems and frustrations and no child is prepared for life unless he is prepared to tolerate them. Therefore, although they do not go out of their way to frustrate their children, or to be unfair to them, they also do not make a big fuss over being unfair at times. They accept these as natural faults of the adult which are necessary to adjust to just as the mean boss' characteristics will also have to be tolerated someday. More importantly, they do not hesitate to apply pressure on their children to teach them that most valuable gift, self-discipline. All the talent in the world, like great wealth, can go down the drain unless used and understood in a mature, disciplined manner. Therefore, they are firm, without being harsh. They may even punish with physical means without being angry. Always uppermost in their mind and heart is the firm belief that the child is getting this spanking because he needs it to learn how to correct his behavior, never because he deserves the pain. And always, physical punishment is used as a last resort after penalties of increasing deprivation have failed.

3. And lastly, the child is always thought well of. He is regarded as a human being who has strengths and weaknesses, often not of our liking, but not blameworthy because of them. If he disappoints his elders, that is their problem, not his. He is never judged by his behavior but instead is viewed as a won-

drous gift, whether he or she pleases us or not. Being pleased depends upon our attitudes, not their behavior, and knowing this, these parents never blame their disappointments on their children, but on their own expectations instead.

As the person of the child is never rejected or questioned, it is fairly easy to see beyond his misbehaviors and also consider his positive aspects. The child never behaves so badly that some good cannot be seen in his other behaviors. Even while being reprimanded for one action, the kind and firm parent has words of praise for the child. He knows he rarely hesitates to criticize the child when the child does something objectionable, and to be fair, he never hesitates to be just as quick with praise and compliments. He knows that what he tells the child, the child will eventually believe. And if he can always see some merit in his son or daughter, that son or daughter will later also be able to see merit in himself or herself. No gift is greater than that of self-acceptance. With it the child can weather any storm, fail any task, and survive any adversity. And should he fail, he only fails; he is not personally crushed as so many people are today and have been throughout history.

Praise and unqualified acceptance of the child can be given constantly, without effort or cost, and its benefits are immense.

No supervisor can follow these three steps at all times in his attempt to be kind and firm. He would have to be perfect to achieve this, and this is impossible. However, this world would most certainly begin changing tomorrow for the better if all peoples would begin to make it a goal at least.

CHAPTER IV

Fears

Along with worry and anger, fear is one of the most commonly felt emotions. Like all emotions, it is created by our own careless thinking, never the environment. Therefore, to correct or diminish a fear, a child or an adult must be taught to question the false ideas they tell themselves just before they become afraid. If these false notions can be successfully challenged, the person will soon calm down even in the midst of a crisis. If they never learn this technique, they can become hysterical over the smallest of issues. Specifically, a person who feels afraid has just told himself 1) something is dangerous which is actually safe, or 2) if it is dangerous one ought to be upset over it. Both of these beliefs are totally irrational. In the first case, we include people who are afraid of the dark, rejection, failure, unpopularity, etc. There can be no harm in any of these because they will never hurt us physically. Secondly, if we should find ourselves in a truly dangerous predicament, the reasons for remaining calm are obvious. What is then called for is a solution to the crisis and this can be achieved so much better when a person has his wits about him. Reacting with fear to the noises of a burglar may cause so much panic the victim may totally forget about calling the police, or looking for a weapon, or a way of escape. As common and natural as it may be to experience fear, the sensible person strives all his life to fight against this tendency because it is so much more efficient and he will furthermore try to teach his children, not only how to overcome fear, but to avoid making themselves afraid in the first place. It is the parent and the teacher, the stories, movies and the television; it is his playmates and his society, all of which teach the child these stupid, regrettable reactions. We are educated to be afraid, and to avoid this we must educate ourselves *not* to be afraid. Let us see how this can be accomplished with our children in managing fears of the dark, people, failure, injury, and rejection and ridicule.

Fears of the Darkness

In truth, the darkness does hold some dangers. It is easy to trip, fall, or bump into objects. These are, strange to say, not the things children fear. It is the imaginary, the non-existent which makes them dread the darkness. The inevitable tales of spooks, ghosts, goblins, and witches are all part of today's normal upbringing. Very few children escape them if they have any association at all with older friends, or brothers and sisters. And of course, we should not leave out the many parents who also cannot hide their genuine fears of the dark. Any child seeing his parent become uncommonly silent while walking through a dark, empty building, or looking behind him in the shadows, sees a perfect example for the child to follow. In this fashion is fear of the dark taught. To overcome it we use the power of logic, over and over again to show the child that what he believes about the dark is simply and utterly not true. This must be practiced until the idea is given up. When it is given up, the fear is gone. It is that simple yet that painstaking.

The particular errors the parent must be aware of are: children must not be frustrated, and children will do as they are told, not as they are shown. The first error will be encountered because the overly kind and too soft parent will not want to push the child into doing something it is afraid of. The best way to overcome a fear is to do the feared activity. Naturally a child will not *want* to expose himself to a dark room, or walk up a dark flight of stairs, he must be made to do these unpleasant tasks against his will. Only by doing them over and over again can he learn they are not dangerous. This involves frustration and mental pain for the child but the intelligent adult nevertheless insists the child expose himself to them, time and again in the certain knowledge that familiarity breeds contempt. The parent or supervisor who refuses to force this frustration on the child will do him no favor as it will leave him with the same fears for years to come. A little immediate relief will otherwise have been exchanged for a lifetime, or at the very least, many months or years of neurotic fear of the dark.

The second error is not as prevalent (a child should do as his parents say, not as they do). Fortunately, most parents outgrow their childhood fears of the dark and thus can set good examples. For those, however, who still have these fears, little can be expected of their children until they master the fear themselves. A mother who scoots under the kitchen table every time it thunders is certain to have little effect in getting her children to be calm during a thunder storm.

Once a child has been thoroughly scared through stories of ghosts and similar nonsense he may prefer to sleep with the light on. This is a fairly common occurrence in some families and can last well into adulthood. To correct such a problem, the parent must be careful not to make fun of the child's fear lest his son or daughter feel the parent has no real understanding of his feelings. All blame should be absolutely avoided since the child adopted the fear through no fault of his own. He is young, impressionable, and lacks the maturity to weigh intellectually what he has been told. Therefore, he has every good reason *for* being afraid of the dark and wanting the light on all night. From *his* point of view he is making perfect sense.

We must show him his point of view is wrong, and then prove it to him by letting him see that nothing happens when the light is switched off. This process of re-education can be time-consuming and have numerous set-backs. However, a persistent attack on the neurotic notions along with the actual experience in the dark will in most instances achieve satisfactory results.

The conversation between an adult and a child who wants the light on all night should ideally go something as follows: "Sonny, let's see if you can't learn to sleep with your bedside light off, all right?"

Eight-year-old Sonny looks scared and says, "No. I get too scared, honest."

"I know you do Sonny, but we can't let this go on forever. You're getting to be a big boy now and we've got to see about teaching you to like the dark."

"I like the dark mom, but not when I'm here alone before I go to sleep."

"What difference does that make. This room is absolutely the same. Putting out the light doesn't change anything does it?"

"Yes it does. It makes scary shadows over there by the window," he said knowingly.

"But Sonny, a shadow can't hurt you. What if it does move back and forth and is shaped strangely, it's only a shadow from the tree outside. *It* isn't scary one bit. That tree out there isn't alive like you and I are. It doesn't know we live here or that you sleep in this bed. It's just an old tree minding its own business and when it gets dark, the light from the street shines against it and throws its shadow on your window. You do the same thing you know when you stand outside at night. Do you become a scary thing all of a sudden?"

"Gee Mom, that's silly, of course not."

"Then why should that tree become scary? Here, let's turn the light off for a few minutes and look at it. See, now the light from the street is shining on the tree and throws the shadows on the window, the floor, and over here on the wall. Isn't it lovely? And we did it by shutting off the light. Now let's turn the light back on and you go to the window to see there's nothing spooky about this whole thing. See the street light? No one is out there. See the tree, it's the same as it always is. That's what you must always tell yourself when you're in the dark: sensible things like, "There are no ghosts or spooks; I'm perfectly safe now, turning off the light doesn't make things dangerous. It's only my thinking they are scary that makes them seem scary. Understand Sonny?"

"Okay mom. You want me to think good things in the dark and then I won't be so afraid."

"Right son. Let's turn the light off again and leave it out even longer this time and tell ourselves sensible things all the while. Then we'll see how scared you get."

In this manner the mother gets the boy to examine critically his belief in the danger of the dark. Never once does she let a chance to challenge his false notions go by. Each time she switches off the light she speaks out loud some of the thoughts she wants him to rehearse to himself when he is alone.

When he becomes comfortable with the light off in the presence of his mother, she can then leave the room briefly so he will be alone in the dark. In a few minutes she can return to switch the light on for the night while praising him liberally for being such a brave boy, and laughing at the silly ideas of spooks. Each succeeding night she will leave him in the dark for a few minutes longer. Again she will return to switch the light on for the night. It can be readily seen that if the child could endure as little as three additional minutes each night he would be tolerating darkness for one hour in twenty days. By that time he will probably be asleep before his mother returns. From time to time Sonny may have a relapse, but if the parent does not lose heart, or blame the child for suddenly falling behind in what he had learned, the loss can quickly be made up if the same procedure is followed. He should continually be reminded of and complimented for his past progress rather than ridiculed or scolded for his present set back. Sonny will be only too quick to blame himself and expect mother's disapproval. This can create nervousness which in turn will make adjusting to the dark that much more difficult.

This same procedure of gradually de-conditioning a child to a fear of the dark can be employed in practically all situations but with slight modifications. Jimmy Holland's folks were in to see me because their seven-year-old boy could not be induced to go into the basement recreation room after his sisters because of a dark section of the stairway and landing at the foot of the stairs. Unless he was carried down by one of his parents he would remain at the top of the stairs and cry.

His parents were advised to follow three steps. 1) Introduce him into the dark area gradually, bit by bit, each day trying to bring him in deeper and have him stay longer. 2) He should be accompanied by mother or father to whom he could turn quickly for protection, relief, or escape from the dark stairs. 3) His false notions about the dark must be challenged continually so that he learns not to frighten himself with thoughts of doom, disaster, and danger. This is most important since without this new mental activity taking place, the child will only be going through the motions of overcoming the dark and will probably endure it only in the company of his folks. Unless the neurotic, alarming thinking can be changed as well, no change is likely to follow.

Mr. Holland was most cooperative in following these suggestions but reported having had some difficulties when we met the following week.

"I took Jimmy to the top of the basement steps every day and just sat down with him talking about the dark and how harmless it was and then I hit on the idea of playing a game. I would switch off the light and we would see who would want to turn the light on first. I lost the first round when I switched it back on after only about fifteen seconds. We had a good laugh over that. The next time, however, Jimmy waited about a minute before he got up and put it on. Eventually that night he was able to sit and chatter with me for about three minutes before he'd lose his nerve. I'd praise him each time for being a brave boy and keep telling him sensible things about the dark.

"I did that for several nights in a row with no further success, until I hit on the idea of making a game out of who could sit on the lowest step while the light was off. He immediately moved two steps from the top while I moved only one. I made a big fuss over him and he just loved it. I could see he was getting real confidence. On our next turn I went to the third step while he, much to my surprise, scooted on down to the fifth. Well that did it. In about thirty seconds he got up like a flash, clambered up the steps past me and cried in fright. I tried to console him and get him right back but it was no use. I tried to reason with him and thought I ought to make him try again before he lost his nerve completely. He wouldn't budge, so I gave up and felt downhearted. He was doing so well. Each time since then I can barely get him to sit on the top step again."

"How do you explain what happened, Mr. Holland?"

"I suppose he got overconfident and wasn't ready to be that far down the steps just then. He needed more time."

"I go along with you there. He simply forgot for a moment how afraid he could be."

"Okay, the damage is done. What do I do now to get him back down?"

"First, let's look at what you could have done in the first place, just in case that happens again. Then we'll talk about what you can do now. This was something that would have been difficult to foresee. Usually a child isn't going to expose himself to more fear than he can usually handle. If anything he won't expose himself to enough. So don't feel badly about that or blame yourself. But you might have turned that incident into a victory for him instead of a defeat if you had instantly praised him for trying the fifth stair in the first place."

"Do you think I regarded it as a defeat? I only wanted him to get back down there before he lost his nerve."

"I'm not questioning your motives Mr. Holland. I'm sure you wanted the best for your boy. However, look at the fuss you immediately made. You must have felt he did wrong or why else would he have to correct what he did by going down into the dark again."

"Yes, I see what you mean. Had I really been satisfied with his going to the fifth step I wouldn't have found anything wrong at all, would I?"

"I doubt it. It's much the same as if you would ask him about the one B on his report card when he has five other A's. Would that sound like you were satisfied, or that you found fault with something?"

"So the poor kid tried his best and I guess I didn't show any real appreciation, not even for his effort. What do I do now?"

"Find several pretexts to praise him in front of his mother or the other children about how much progress he made the first week. Show him quite honestly that this failure makes absolutely no difference to you as far as your love for him goes. Then take him to the basement steps again and start all over. Make a joke out of how eager he was the first week and caution him to go slower this week. Unless I'm very much mistaken he'll start slowly but soon catch up to where he was."

Mr. Holland reported in a week that Jimmy had reached the bottom of the steps as long as his dad was on the stairway. He had already planned to start from the top again this next week but to have Jimmy be by himself, all the while telling himself that it was fun to play games in the dark, there was nothing to be afraid of, and anytime he wanted to he could always turn around and run up the stairs, switch on the light and stand beside daddy.

"You have the principles well in mind Mr. Holland. Try them and see what happens." Several weeks later he called to report that Jimmy was practically over his fear of the basement steps and was gaining enough confidence from this victory to gain greater self-assurance in other areas of his life.

The essential steps which corrected this condition were a gradual introduction to the dark, at first in the presence of an adult, later alone, and a constant challenging of his false ideas of the danger of the darkness. Mr. Holland was kind to Jimmy even when he faltered (with the one exception) but he was firm and insisted the boy must face his fear even if it were measured in seconds or inches. He was careful not to make that common mistake of believing children must not be frustrated.

The use of logic and persuasion cannot be underestimated in helping children overcome their fears. I once had occasion to work with a six-year-old girl who abruptly began to wake up nightly with the most fearful and anxious feelings imaginable. She would be in a cold sweat, walk around in great agitation, sometimes scream in terror, and looked for all the world like she were being chased by ghosts.

The first mental health worker who interviewed the parents and the child learned that Betty had been sleeping with her grandfather and it was concluded that this caused so much unconscious guilt and fear of her incestuous sexual feelings that she could not tolerate the nearness of his body and that this caused her to escape through the panic reaction.

I had strong doubts about this interpretation since the child had been sleeping with grandfather some time before the symtoms appeared. Other explanations needed to be found. In speaking to the girl it was soon learned that she lived across the street from a cemetery and that on one night prior to the first night of terror, Betty was scared about stories of the dark and the ghosts from the cemetery by her girl friend, a child slightly older than Betty. On the assumption that this was the cause of her nightly panic I proceeded to explain to her that there were no such thing as ghosts, that her girl friend was pulling her leg, and that Betty ought to go over to her house and tell her to go jump in the lake. Never for one moment did I let up from this approach in all of our five sessions. After the second meeting we immediately began to see a lessening of the symptoms and this, of course, only spurred me on more forcefully to challenge her beliefs that the dark was dangerous and that she would be disturbed and hurt by goblins. Two years later I checked up on Betty again and found that she had had only two more nights of having bad dreams and, furthermore, she willingly left her grandfather's bed to sleep by herself. The change was astounding, quick, and lasting.

The parent may want to know what a conversation with such a child is like, and whether it can be duplicated by other guardians who have similar problems with their children. Here is somewhat how it goes.

"You let that girl scare you? How silly. Don't you know she's just trying to have fun with you? Why there is no such thing as a ghost. There never was such a thing as a ghost and there never will be. Can you understand that? Repeat after me. 'There is no such thing as ghosts. My girl friend is full of baloney. I'm not going to listen to her ever again. The next time she starts with that ghost stuff I'm going to tell her to stop it or I'll go home.' "

This argument was presented forcefully and all of her questions were answered truthfully and directly. I also used my position of prestige to the fullest advantage and asked her to decide who knew more, her friend or I. But more importantly, I simply hammered away at her belief until she could begin to entertain different notions. And I further assured her that when people die, they stay dead and never rise to bother anyone. "Now, if you want to be foolish and work yourself up into a sweat every night, you can just go on believing that garbage your friend gave you. But, Betty, if you want to sleep peacefully, just remember what I said and keep telling yourself over and over that there is no such thing as ghosts, that just because it's dark outside you're not going to be attacked, and that your silly girl friend can scare herself if she wants to, but you've had enough of it." In this manner, and in many variations on the same theme she recovered almost completely in a short time, much to her relief and that of her distraught parents.

CHAPTER V

Fear of People

All neurotic conditions are regrettable, but one of the most pathetic of these is shyness. The boy or girl who has a fear of people is doomed to a particular kind of unhappiness. Most pronounced, of course, is loneliness. A shy child may have its family to socialize with, or perhaps a close friend or two. Any attempts to leave these safe harbors for unchartered seas is almost bound to wind up in solitary shipwreck. More's the pity, for people are basically not hostile, they tend towards civility. Few are physically dangerous, and most want companionship as much as the shy child does. Yet, there he stands amidst a population of people many of whom could be hospitable, even very friendly. But the shy child is so conditioned against making the necessary overtures to let these people know him that he starves for companionship in the midst of plenty. This is the truly neurotic aspect of this problem.

What is the cause of this regrettable attitude of mind? And how can it be corrected? The answer to the first question is usually a strong inferiority complex. These children feel so insignificant they are certain in their own minds that others would not want anything to do with them. Their silent sentences go something like this: "I'm no good. I don't like myself. What would anyone else want with a worthless good-for-nothing like me? I'm sure people can see how stupid I am and that's why they stay away from me. And I can't blame them either."

This feeling of inferiority may arise in numerous ways, but when viewed at a distance we see two common sources. The first is the indoctrination the child has gotten from his society that he is no good unless he is perfect in all respects. His insecure parents have probably pointed out every mistake he has ever made, have blamed him for making them and have withheld their approval of him until he could improve. Secondly, they have unwittingly taught him that he must have the approval of other people or he is even more worthless. To these parents worthwhileness is not something a person has at all times and is totally independent from outside influence, it is what *others* think of them. For this reason they see themselves and their children as lesser human beings when they are not getting praise from others, and are, therefore, very sensitive about other people's opinion and must drive themselves to recapture their good graces.

A second way in which a child may become shy is through imitating his parents. If they are withdrawn, the child is not likely to get the experience or push he needs to mingle freely with others. He may find comfort and relief only when in familiar surroundings and with familiar people. This can set the pattern of shyness. His reluctance to be forward will leave him excluded by his school mates or neighbors and he then in turn interprets this incorrectly to mean he is different and not as good as they, and so they leave him alone. Again we are back to the inferiority feelings. Of course, not every adult or child who likes to be by himself is doing so for neurotic reasons. Often, a gifted or creative person simply finds little companionship with others because his interests or intelligence are so foreign to those with whom he must associate. Rather than be bored, he prefers his own company to theirs. Instead of feeling inferior, he may quite rightly believe himself to be superior.

The difference between these two kinds of isolated persons is this: the neurotically shy child will almost always feel inferior whether he's with superior or even inferior persons. The creative, socially isolated person can blossom forth quite readily and be warm, comfortable, and outgoing the moment he finds himself in the proper environment. He is a fish out of water who can swim perfectly normally the moment he is put back in his element. The truly shy child is a fish who is afraid to swim at all, unless it be in a small, well-tended fish bowl in the home of his parents.

The correction of neurotic shyness must pursue three steps: 1) the beliefs of having to be perfect, and having to be approved of by others must be shown to him to be false; 2) his parents must set better examples of mingling freely with people; and 3) they must force him to perform the fearful actions over and over again until he no longer fears them. It is possible in some instances for this correction to take place solely by fulfiilling step one: overcoming the false beliefs which maintain the fear of people. In most instances however, parents will actively have to assist in the correction process by not committing Error Number Five (Children Learn More From What Their Parents Say Than From What They Do), and Error Number Seven (Children Must Not Be Frustrated).

Jane Cummings was fifteen years old and had been a painfully shy girl since she entered school at the age of six. She was not an unattractive girl although she was not beautiful either. The assets she did have were completely hidden by the pathetic and sorry way she carried herself. She entered the office with her back hunched, her eyes downcast and looked for all the world like a whipped pup wtih its tail between its legs.

Very shortly after telling me of her problem of loneliness she broke out in tears. She reported being miserable around people but wanting very much to be one of the group. Her explanation for not being accepted by her peers was her poverty. Though her clothes were neat and clean they were seconds. She lived in a shack at the edge of town and preferred walking to school rather than have her father drive her on cold mornings in his jalopy. The contrast between her family car and the newer models the other children were chauffered in was too great she thought. She went on to report how inferior she felt, how people made her nervous, how she could not look them in the face because she would blush, and that walking home after school, always alone, was the only time, outside of her home, she felt real relief.

I began by trying to show her that her poverty had nothing to do with her shyness. Instead it was her attitude toward her clothes, car, and house, which made her feel inferior and different. If we could get her to *think* differently about those things she would *feel* differently, too.

"But changing my attitude," she protested quickly, "isn't going to change my clothes, is it?"

"Certainly not Jane. Is that why you've come to see me, to give you better clothes and give your father a newer car?"

"No, I know you can't do that. But that's why I doubt you can help me. If I were as well-off as other kids, I wouldn't feel so self-conscious don't you see?"

"It's true you might get over your shyness if you suddenly got rich. And for your sake I hope your father strikes an oil well in his back yard. However, suppose he doesn't. Does that mean you're doomed forever to feeling you're not as good as others?"

"Yes, it does, as long as we're *this* poor at least."

"Oh I see, your value as a person is determined by how much money you have."

"Not entirely of course. But when you're as poor as we are that's different."

"No it isn't Jane. If we accept your thinking we have to accept it all the way. Either money makes you better or it doesn't. According to you a person making $10,000 a year is twice as good as someone making $5,000. Which means that everyone ought to feel inferior most of the time since there are very few millionaires compared to the rest of us who make less. Does that make sense?"

"That's not what I mean. A person should have a *certain* amount of money. Then they can feel good about themselves. You know, not feel like they're failures."

"But your father is only a failure as a wage-earner, that doesn't mean he's a failure as a person does it?"

"I'm not blaming my father. He can't help it. He dropped out of high school, then got injured while truck driving. That's why we're on welfare."

"Then wouldn't you say he has good reason for not being a good provider? After all he hardly enjoys the standard of living he's givng his family does he?"

"Nevertheless doctor, he's still thought of as a failure by other people."

"And why shouldn't he be. After all he is a failure as a provider. Does that mean he's a rotten person because he's a rotten provider?"

"Other people seem to think so."

"That's their problem. What happened to your father is unfortunate but proves nothing about his value to himself or your value to yourself."

"You don't agree then that I have a reason to feel self-conscious around girls who dress better than I do or who can go to parties or on trips?"

"Certainly not. The only reason you feel so self-conscious around them is because you're telling yourself ridiculous things when you get around them. What, for example, do you tell yourself when you see a group of girls at school?"

"Oh that's easy. I think of how much they have and how they must look down on me for what I have. I'm sure they don't want anything to do with someone who is so poor she has to accept welfare."

"So you then conclude you're not as good as they are."

"Yes. That's exactly how I feel."

"And that last idea is the neurotic belief you have. Unless you show yourself just how foolish it is you'll always feel inferior, unless of course you get money someday."

"But it's *not* foolish."

"Then prove to me how you lose value just because you're not as well-dressed as they are."

"I don't know how to prove it. I just know it."

"Rubbish, Jane. You're just believing that because you're unthinkingly giving yourself that propaganda all the time. I'll show you what I mean. You're in the choir I understand. Now would you say you're a better, more worthwhile person than some girl who can't carry a melody and therefore can't join the choir?"

"No of course not."

"Right. In other words she has no value to the choir master but she can still be valuable to herself."

"And she might be very good at other things besides singing."

"Fine. Now why doesn't this same thinking apply to you? It may be true you have no value to some girls who can dress up in all the latest fashions, but what has that to do with your value to *you* not to mention the other skills and talents you have?"

She, like most of my patients, kept insisting that her shortcoming was somehow "different," but I kept on insisting it was the same. "If you would stop insisting you're a crumb just because you can't keep up with the school fashion-plates you'll soon stop feeling inferior."

"But that won't change my clothes or make me more acceptable will it?"

"It might since most people aren't the harsh judges you think they are. Even if they still snubbed you, what difference would that make if you didn't let the whole thing bother you in the first place?"

"Oh I see what you mean," she declared finally with insight. "If I don't *let* them bother me, and I still can't dress better,

I'll still feel fine because I have *made* myself feel better and that's what I'm really concerned with in the first place isn't it? And that's why you *can* help me even if you can't change my other problems about being poor."

Here she had it in a nutshell. However, she found putting her thinking into practice a harder task than she realized. In the following weeks she often felt depressed because she felt she was no more liked than before, despite the fact that she was trying very hard to talk herself out of the self-blaming she had been doing. It was easy to determine that by and large she still was doing little about overcoming her detachment towards people. She still avoided groups at school, walked home alone, and blushed when she had to recite in class.

Only a massive dose of assignments, geared to expose her to this feared activity could eventually make her feel so at home with them they would no longer constitute a problem. I instructed her and her parents to make greater efforts at having face-to-face, or at least voice-to-voice contacts.

"Jane," I told her one day, "from now on I want you to answer the telephone at home each time, and I want you to answer the door. Your folks have agreed to let you do this. I also want you to invite someone each week to have dinner at your house, to ask someone to sleep over with you once a month, to carry on a conversation with one of your neighbors for at least fifteen minutes each day. When the family goes out to a drive-in or to a movie, I want you to take charge and order the meals and pay for them; the same with the movie tickets. Anytime you see one of your schoolmates I want you to introduce them to your family, or if you're alone I want you to go up and talk to them about anything. You need practice at this business of facing and talking to others and the only way you'll get it is by assigning yourself these tasks. You can think of others as you go along."

"Oh I can't do all those things doctor, I'll blush terribly. They'll laugh at me and think I'm silly."

"Well Jane you have to admit it is funny and silly, being afraid of people who won't hurt you. Anyway, when you think you're going to blush just convince yourself that that's *your* problem and since no one is perfect you're entitled to it. If they get upset about you that's *their* problem and if they don't like you, so what. You don't *need* their friendship anyway."

"But I do need it."

"You don't have it now. If you needed it as you say, and hadn't gotten it all this time, you'd be dead wouldn't you?"

"Well I didn't mean I'd die if they didn't like me, I just. . . ."

"Oh but that's the point, you *do* believe that you'll die, or be just as miserable as death. That's why you get so upset when they snub you. You've let it mean too much to you. When you learn to relax and not take every person's rebuff *personally*, then you'll find some people will like you very much. Why? Because you won't be running away anymore but will be letting *them* know you want to be friends."

"You mean that I'm a loner mainly because I keep myself away from people who really might like me?"

"Absolutely Jane. Put yourself in their shoes. Would you try to make friends with a girl that never talks to you, or who looks awfully uncomfortable every time she looks at you. And when you see how much she prefers to be by herself, would you make any effort to get chummy with her?"

"But I don't want to avoid talking to others or be by myself. I can't help it!"

"*I* understand that Jane. How do you expect *them* to know this. They believe what they see not the silent wishes you keep to yourself. They can't *see* your wishes can they?"

"So I must *let* them know I want to be friends by doing this homework, and once I convince them I really want to be friendly I'll make more friends."

This did the trick. The groundwork toward getting her over her perfectionism had been prepared, the homework was assigned and the reasons for it understood, and now the insight was gained that people avoided her partly because of her lack of interest in them. Combined, they enabled her to appy herself over the following months in getting over her fear of people. In one of our last sessions she reported, "It's so wonderful not to have to look at the ground all the time anymore, wondering if a boy or girl is looking me over and thinking whether I'm good enough for them. Lots of great people were poor and they didn't let their backgrounds hold them back; Abraham Lincoln for example."

"And have you found out that the earth won't open and swallow you up just because someone doesn't approve of you?"

"Definitely" she laughed. "I went to a dance last week and was asked onto the floor by two fellows. Of course I know that's nothing special, but for me it is. I can remember when I wouldn't go to a dance at all."

"How do you suppose those fellows felt about you?"

"I hope they liked me. I tried to be nice and friendly also. If they didn't, well I'm not perfect and still need more practice at being social. So I'll just have to attend more dances, or take a few lessons, or get more experience in keeping conversation going. I'll do it too, someday. But most of all, I think the one idea that helped me the most was that other people weren't snubbing me because there was anything wrong with me, but rather because I didn't make much of an effort to be friendly myself. After all, if I don't do something to *show* them I want to be friendly, why should they make the effort? All along I was expecting something from them which I wouldn't do myself."

It was still a long hard pull for Jane. Relapses occurred during the remainder of high school, but with the kind but firm urging of her parents and school counselor, and the use of a rational way of thinking she could bring herself out of these slumps until she gained enough self-confidence to be an unnoticeable, normal adolescent.

CHAPTER VI

Fear of Failure

In this perfectionistic, neurotic society, one of the worst doctrines we teach our children is the one that goes: if it is worth doing, it must be done well. Another variation of this theme goes like this: be the best at whatever you do; never play second fiddle; you're great if you win and inferior if you lose. All of these philosophies, although quite noble sounding, are actually the death knell to eager, spontaneous, and healthy trial and error. Combined they create for millions of people a very common fear, the fear of failure.

If we regard failure as shameful proof of our worthlessness we will naturally work feverishly not to fail. We will thereby make it equivalent to a life-and-death issue. Once it reaches these proportions we are loathe to undertake anything unless it already has a good chance of succeeding. All other activities will be avoided. Eventually such a narrowing of interest and participation in life will take place that we will do *only* those things we do well.

The startled parent must not conclude from this that our wishes, desires, and strivings for success, or fame, or betterment are neurotic and to be discouraged. Wishing, and working hard, very hard to fulfill these wishes is sane and healthy. All of us are being perfectly normal to want success, to do well at our tasks, even to wish to be the greatest ping pong player in the world. Only by having dreams and working toward them can our fondest wishes come true.

However, one can wish too much. When our desires become so strong that we believe they *must* be fulfilled, then it is no longer a wish at all but a necessity. Whenever desires become demands a change from the healthy to the unhealthy has been made. The case of Ben, a seventeen-year-old high school drop-out is a case in point. His parents had urged him on in his high school studies for years to no avail. He took the matter lightly and in time became so bored with his studies that he dropped out of school entirely. For almost a year he worked at a half dozen jobs, each harder, more menial than the next. The big holiday he expected to have from being freed of school's drudgery did not materialize, needless to say, and as he neared his eighteenth birthday he confessed his error to his parents and asked if they would send him to business school to be a bookkeeper. Mr. and Mrs. Williams were indeed pleased with this turn of attitude of Ben's but such an education would strain the family's short finances. Finally it was decided to send the boy on the one condition that the first sign of failure, laziness, or indifference would mean dismissal.

Ben went to business school *determined* to succeed. Not only did his now mature sense of obligation not to waste the family's hard-earned money drive him forward, but the realization as well that this might very well be his last chance to bring himself out of the untrained labor market.

He ran into immediate trouble on his first examinations. Though he had studied carefully for several nights he barely passed, being so tense and fearful of what the consequences would be if he did not do well. With each following test, his anxiety mounted until he took hours to do homework and continued doing badly on his tests. His parents would have dropped their support at this point but for the fact that they could well see how he had earnestly studied and how in addition their son needed help at this point for his "nerves" and depression. He was referred for psychotherapy.

"It beats me doctor," he said introducing his problem, "how I can do so badly on these tests when I've studied the material so well. Something happens to me so that I just freeze up and my mind goes blank. And I know what it is only I can't do a thing about it."

"You think you know what it is?"

"Sure. I'm so nervous I can't think straight. All I keep thinking about is how important it is to pass with a good grade and then I feel myself getting so nervous I just don't remember a thing. And when I see *that* happening I practically get panicky because I know what flunking out means to me."

Here was an example of a pateint who had uncommon insight into his problem. Yet, good as it was, his insight was incomplete.

"Ben, you're right about what makes you do so poorly on tests, namely your anxiety over possibly failing, but tell me what makes your anxiety in the first place?"

"I just told you, I'm afraid I'm going to fail."

"No Ben, not quite. You said your mind becomes a blank when you get tense taking a test. That part is true. However, what brings on the tension? It's not the test, or the possibility that you might fail the test. You might fail, therefore, that belief is a perfectly sound, healthy belief and can't cause your tension. It's only your false, irrational, unprovable beliefs which can upset you."

"False beliefs," he said questioningly. "I haven't believed anything that wasn't true. I have to get good grades or I won't pass. Is that a false belief?"

"No, but you've been saying something else to yourself which you're not aware of which is utterly false."

"What's that?"

"That you *have* to pass."

Ben looked as though he were ready to leave. "What's unhealthy about that? That's the first sensible thought I've had in years. That's what my folks tried to drill into my head for years, only I wouldn't listen," he said with open irritation.

"Perhaps so Ben, but it's still an unhealthy, false belief. Prove to me you have to pass this bookkeeping course."

"I won't amount to anything if I don't, that's why."

"You may be right. Now, tell me why you *must* amount to something."

"Because I don't want to wind up as a bum."

"Of course you don't. Does that prove you *can't* become a bum, simply because you don't *want* to be one? In other words would you say that you mustn't or can't die because you don't *want* to die? Obviously not. Yet, that's what you're saying about being a bookkeeper. What you should be telling yourself about these tests is that you want very much to pass and justify your folks' money and faith in you, but that it is hardly a *necessity* to pass. After all you will survive if you flunk out won't you?"

"Sure I'll survive, but . . ."

"Okay, then its *not* a necessity to pass. It will simply mean you won't get everything you want. Then all you can do is try again at something else. Getting terribly upset over failing doesn't correct the failure does it? If you won't blame yourself for failing, like yourself through thick and thin, then you won't be neurotically upset over your lack of perfection and you will calmly try something else. If you blame and hate yourself, rather than hate just the fact that you have failed at *some thing*, then you will be too disturbed to correct your failure because you'll be too busy calling yourself a lot of awful names. If that's going to be your focus, then the problem and why you failed will *not* be the focus. And if *that* isn't getting any attention, how do you expect to correct it?' '

"You expect me not to be upset over flunking out a second time?"

"Certainly, and you will, too, if you'll stop to realize that the very disturbance you feel so justified in harboring will be the main cause of your failing."

"You're saying that I *will* flunk out if I become upset over the possibility of flunking."

"Sure. That's what you've been doing so far. Your wish to pass has become so strong that it's no longer just a wish, it's a necessity."

"So what, is that bad?"

"Its not good Ben because its impossible to be perfect. If you believe you must get passing grades you're bound to be upset when you don't live up to that perfectionistic demand. Anytime you change your healthy wishes into neurotic demands you're in trouble. It's like what happens when we freeze water. Let the unfrozen water represent your wish to pass this course. As we increase the coldness of the water by small degrees it soon hits the freezing point. Then we have water, just as we did before, but its form has changed considerably. For one thing, in the state of ice it is painful to hold, or it can be thrown like a rock. It's the same with your wish to pass. As it becomes stronger by degrees, it reaches a point where it is a demand, a necessity. It's the same thing it was before, yet it's different. It's no longer a healthy thing, it's neurotic."

"So if I don't make a need out of my wish to pass these tests, I'll pass them?"

"Not necessarily, but you're more likely to pass because you won't be anxious beforehand and that will permit you to put down on paper whatever you've learned. Try this as an experiment: the next time you take a test keep telling yourself you want to pass it and you'll try your best. Also tell yourself that you don't have to pass it since the world won't come to an end, and if you should do poorly at it it'll simply mean you'll have to study what went wrong and what you could do next time not to make the same mistakes. Under no condition should you blame yourself for not being perfect because you will feel so badly you won't ever get back to studying your mistakes which caused the poor grades."

"Doctor, I just thought of another example and I want you to tell me if it fits what you've been telling me. When I was a kid I had to recite a poem in front of the class. At home, by myself, I recited it perfectly, apparently because I wasn't making myself anxious by insisting it had to be perfect. No one was listening so I stayed relaxed and did a good job. When I got in front of the classroom I got nervous and fumbled several times because I told myself I had to do it perfectly. If I had taken the same relaxed attitude in the classroom as I did at home, that I didn't *have* to do it letter perfect, I might have done it without a mistake. So if I take a test the same way and not be so afraid I may fail, I'll do much better because I won't be changing my wish to pass into a need to pass."

This was the crux of the problem. Ben saw it clearly but it remained for time to see how he could apply it. Two weeks after this initial session he had a test and reported his progress to me the third week.

"I didn't do too badly Dr. Hauck. I could sure see what you meant about how I was sabotaging myself. I took special notice to see what I was thinking just before and during the test and I caught myself several times telling myself I had to do well or I'd flunk out and what would I do then, and what would my folks say, or, well, you know, all kinds of things. I could practically feel my tension rise when I had those thoughts. So I tried what you said and questioned them. Did I have to pass? Would it really be the end of the world? Did I have to be a bookkeeper? Who says I wouldn't do better at something else? So I'm not perfect, who is? I kept thinking this sort of thing and although I was not as calm as I wished I would be, still I passed the test with a C, so I know I can do it, and is that ever a relief! Frankly I wouldn't have believed this until it happened. Emotions can sure play heck with you."

"Not all emotions Ben," I corrected him. "It's the negative

emotions you want to control, not the positive, happy, light-hearted feelings. Negative emotions and the ability to think clearly cannot exist side by side. You're either in one state or the other. It's like oil and water, they don't mix."

Ben passed his next test with another C. Nothing succeeds like success so it was becoming easier to be relaxed which in turn brought out an occasional B and soon he was relaxed enough to do straight B work and pass his course comfortably.

The beliefs that one must be competent in all things or that failure is disgraceful are among the strongest and silliests notions we teach our children. We have taught them to compare themselves against the performances of others and to conclude they are worthless if they fall short of the goal which they have come to believe is not just desirable but essential.

The wise counselor will make it a point to train the child at every opportunity never to blame himself for his shortcomings or outright failures. Instead he will encourage him to do better if he can and to accept his shortcoming if he can't. If your youngster clumsily breaks your favorite vase or loses your tools and he looks like he's going to cry over the loss, assure him he needn't blame himself. Say something reassuring to him like: "Don't blame yourself Johnny. You're not perfect. I don't like what you did but I always like you anyway. Now let's see what we can do to teach you to be more careful. In the past several weeks you've had several such accidents. I don't think you're doing much about being more careful or else you wouldn't make all these simple mistakes. Suppose I take away your Saturday night movie this week. Do you suppose that would help you be more aware of your actions?"

Here we see a parent who loves his child unconditionally, and who regards the behavior as bad, not the *child*. He is calm about this situation because he regards it as a problem no different from any other problem. He will try a minor penalty first. If this does not work he will increase the penalty in the same kindly way he imposed the restriction on the movie.

The fear of failure is such a common occurrence that we could well benefit by looking at another case study. Eileen Prentis, a bright sixteen-year-old high school debater was referred to me by her school counselor. She had been, for several months, becoming increasingly tense before a debate and was now so nervous that she sometimes vomited before a debate and was having many fitful nights during which she slept very poorly.

"I think it all started when Larry Cronin joined the debate squad this year," she said during our first session. "He's very good at public speaking, you know, forceful, self-assured, pounds the table if he wants to make a point; that sort of thing. Well, next to Larry I'm not doing so well, and before he joined I was thought very highly of as a debater. They even voted me as captain of the debating squad this year. I'm trying to live up to that honor but I know I can't because Larry is simply better than I am."

Knowing that she was demanding great competence from herself and not getting it I ventured to make an interpretation to her. "Have you felt nervous, depressed, and disgusted with yourself knowing that you'll accomplish only a second-best performance?"

"I certainly have. I've done everything I know of to speak more persuasively but the thought that one of the members of my squad is better than the captain of the squad, well it's just horribly humiliating."

"Sounds to me Eileen that you believe you must be perfect or you're despicable."

"No, I don't want to be perfect. Nobody is that. But I think I should be tops on the squad or I shouldn't have the honor of being captain."

"Would you feel the same if you weren't captain?"

"I suppose so. I'm terribly competitive and if I don't do my best at whatever I do, I'm miserable for days."

"I thought so" I agreed. "So we get back to my initial point;

either you're tops and a great gal, or you're down here in the mud and you're no good."

I proceeded to show her the ABC's of emotions, that her *attitudes* toward being second best were causing her mental distress, not her slightly inferior ability to debate. My line of reasoning went something like this: "Eileen, whether you see it now or not you must eventually see that you're a perfectionist of the worst sort. You believe you become a better person when you do things better than others. That's totally false. As long as you believe that nonsense you'll always be upset when someone beats you at some skill."

She protested that what she could do or could not do *was* an accurate reflection of the kind of person she was.

"Nonsense," I replied. "Do you mean to say that you loathe, detest, and blame the other members of the squad when they come in second or third, or last for that matter?"

"No of course I don't. That's different."

"*What's* different about it? You're saying when they debate poorly they're still fine kids but poor debaters. When you debate poorly you believe you're a poor debater (which temporarily may be true), *and* that you're a good-for-nothing, worthless slob. What makes you so different from everyone else? Do you think you're so special that you can't judge yourself like you judge others? I'd say you're being conceited. Really conceited!"

"Me conceited? I've been feeling terribly inferior. That's not conceit."

"It certainly is when you become all upset because you somehow believe you're supposed to be God's gift to the debating society. Don't you see the basic conceit in that? You actually believe you can't fail in any way and that's impossible. Everybody fails at most things at some times. It's not awful to fail. It can't be helped. Only superhumans do things right the first time, all the time. Failing at anything only proves you're either inexperienced or ungifted at that task. You don't play the oboe do you? No? Well, would you say you're worthless, inferior, or bad because you're a lousy oboe player? Of course not. You're still a fine person even though you're a poor oboe player. And you don't sing opera either do you? So are you an awful person because you're an awful opera singer?"

"I know what you're going to say next" she interrupted. "I'm still a fine person even though I'm not a fine debater."

"Right you are Eileen. And if you really understand that you can't be upset because you're second on the squad since you'll like yourself anyway. Then you won't be upsetting yourself neurotically and will be better able to do something about improving your debating skills. For this next week I want you to challenge very vigorously those false ideas you've had about having to be the best, or being worthless if you aren't tops, or how terrible it is to fail once in a while. Really fight these ideas. Debate them with yourself and show yourself each time that they are truly false. Then you'll relax and this neurotic vomiting and poor sleeping will surely diminish."

A great deal of the world's misery would vanish if we could get people to stop placing impossible standards upon themselves, standards which are more appropriate to gods than humans. We are basically being conceited and grandiose when we believe we must act like superhumans rather than like the fallible humans which we are. Being just poor human beings we *must* fail, we botch up things, we *must* do wrong. We have no choice in the matter. But if we will not blame ourselves for our failures and instead *study* our mistakes carefully, then we can probably do better *next* time. If we blame ourselves, our attention is not really on the mistake at all, or on how we made it, or on how we might improve. When we blame ourselves our attention is only on what useless, worthless, bad, and wicked people we are for having failed in the first place. We accept the seasons, the roundness of the earth, death, and taxes. Why and when will we accept our own humanity? When will we realize that we learn *by* making mistakes and *then* improving on them? As I often point out to my patients:

"Everything in this office was perfected through trial and error. The steel in the desk, the window, the plaster, the books, etc. When these people first made these things the quality was poor indeed. And if they had blamed themselves for making an imperfect product they would have said, 'This was badly done. I'm no good. I'll never be able to do better. I'm giving up.' No, instead they said, 'This batch of tile turned out badly. Too bad. What did I do and what can I change so the *next* batch of tile will be better?' And they tried perhaps many times before a good finished product was achieved."

Rather than insist of our children that everything they do must be done well, let's encourage them to do it even if it will turn out badly. No more fear of failure, mistakes, or poor performance. A child armed with this philosophy will undertake numerous tasks, and, being unnervous about the outcome, will do better than he would otherwise. Equally as important, he will at least have tried. This means practice. The more he practices (in contrast to giving up because his first attempt was not a smashing success) the sooner he will eventually *improve.* It is far more important *to do* than *to do well.* Few of us can do well at the start, but practically all of us can do better as we gain practice and experience. If we expect perfection right off, the necessary practice which can eventually lead to mastery will be missing. And missing this, mastery seldom follows.

CHAPTER VII

Fear of Injury

Children seem to make a great deal out of their injuries because they haven't the experience to determine their seriousness. We must expect them to cry over their hurts, certainly. We can even expect them to become temporarily hysterical or panicky over a bleeding wound, or very strange bodily sensation. Frequently, however, children have a way of regarding these, and many lesser injuries as though they all required hospitalization. This catastrophizing should be controlled for the good of their emotional development lest they be allowed to think unrealistically about future injuries. A child who cuts his knee while roller skating may build it so far out of proportion that he fears roller skating again. If this restriction of his activity could be confined only to the skating, a great deal of harm would not be done, although that in itself would be regrettable enough. It is the tendency for other sports to become feared as well as skating wherein the damage lies. Should this tendency toward playing it safe spread (as neurotic habits often do) to activities other than sports, such as driving a car, taking a plane ride, or standing on a ladder, we can easily see how incapacitated the person can become. Such narrowing of one's life space can progress to the point where the child is doing *only* those things which he feels are absolutely safe.

Shaming a child out of his fear, or appealing to his maturity, "Big boys don't cry," can certainly work. These methods, however, lack the conviction the child needs to be truly unafraid. He may well get back on his bike or try his roller skates again, and *if* he is successful all will go smoothly. But if he should have another fall he is likely to become more upset and feel badly about himself for letting dad down and for being such a sissy. This is not the soil in which self-confidence and mastery grow.

It is far better to reason with the child to show him, 1) the injury is not as bad as he imagines, and 2) even if he might get hurt, he is better off taking a chance since he will learn the skill sooner or later rather than playing it safe since life will be poorly rewarding unless he risks his safety from time to time.

Ten-year-old Mary developed school phobia and her puzzled mother brought her to see me. Mary was an A student, but since starting the fourth grade with a strict teacher her interest in school wanned rapidly until she refused to attend at all. It seems that this teacher had the habit of slapping the faces of those boys she felt were making no effort to get the work. Mary was shocked at this practice and soon feared she would be next if her work should ever prove unsatisfactory. To bring in perfect homework each night required only two hours of study at the most. Her fears, however, slowed her down with constant doubts until she needed until bedtime to do the same satisfactory work. Even then she could not attend classes the following day with a light heart. The slightest sign of disapproval by the teacher toward anyone of the students was noted very keenly by Mary who then resolved to study even harder that night so she would be sure never to be at the receiving end of the teacher's anger.

I agreed with Mary that her teacher could certainly have handled her class in better ways but wondered why she worried over such treatment since she was such a conscientious student. She replied that she was so scared of possibly being treated that way, she would do anything to make certain it never happened. I then pointed out that her excessive fear of being reprimanded verbally, or even with a slap on the face, was preventing her from concentrating to such a degree that she was now more in danger than ever before of being treated exactly in this fashion. It was quite clear to me Mary would have to lose her fear of injury and pain before she could reapply herself to her work .Then she could perform well and avoid her teacher's wrath.

"Mary, perhaps it is true that your teacher may slap you one of these days. I still don't see why you have to be so upset over that."

"I don't want her to slap me and I know she's going to," was her reply.

"I'm sure you don't want her to slap you and I think it would be odd if you thought anything else. But look, honey, it isn't the slap that's upsetting you since you haven't even been touched yet. It's the thought of being hit that's making you afraid. You're probably telling yourself it would be awful if the teacher hit you; it would hurt terribly; you couldn't stand it; it would be so embarrassing, and so on."

"That's right. I'm really afraid of her."

"Should you be?"

She did not answer this question. In fact, for the remainder of the hour she barely said anything. Whether she thought I did not understand her problem, or whether I was taking the side of the teacher I do not know. However, because she was listening I continued to reason with her even though she barely joined in.

"I don't see why you have to be afraid of her at all Mary. Sure she can hurt you, but how much is she likely to do? From what you've told me she never does any more than just that. She doesn't beat on the kids, or tramp all over them. Just a slap now and then and a scolding. I'm sure your parents have done that much before, if not even more. Yet you aren't fearful of going home to your family each day are you? The way you describe this woman it's like she practically kills the kids."

"But she hurts them." she insisted.

"Sure, but for how long? Does that slap hurt all day?" No answer. "Does it sting for half a day? One Hour? A few minutes? How long Mary?" No answer. "I seriously doubt that it would last more than a few minutes. So even if this awful thing did happen to you it would only last a matter of maybe five minutes at the most. Now, how much would it hurt? Is it as bad as breaking a leg?" She shook her head. "No? Then is it as bad as cutting yourself? No? Is it like skinning your knee when you fall off your bike?"

"Yes I think it would sting like that?"

"All right Mary, now think back. Do you always cry when you fall and hurt yourself? I doubt that you do. In fact, I'm pretty sure that you often don't even care about the bruise and go right back to riding your bike or roller skating. You don't keep telling yourself, 'Oh, that hurt terribly. I'm never, never going to ride my bike or skate again ever.' "

"No I don't."

"Why not? You've just been saying the pain of being slapped is so awful you dread going back to school but the same pain you get from falling from a bike doesn't bother you and you go right back for more. Why can it scare you one time and not the other?" She did not answer but it was plain to see she was studying the question.

"I'll tell you why. It's because you keep telling yourself quite foolishly that you can't stand a pain if your teacher gives it to you on the face but you could stand it if you gave it to yourself. And because you believe this you get upset. You must think about this carefully and see that they're the same and if you're not upset over one you certainly don't have to be upset over the other."

And so it went. Not only for the rest of that hour, but over the next several weeks I hammered this logic home until she was quite prepared for the teacher's injuries if and when they might come. She learned to fear her less and less and decided a slap in the face was not impossible to bear. This permitted her to relax about her school work which made her more efficient and it could be done in an hour's time. Not only was it done quicker but better, thus removing her still further from the actual probability of being hit. This could not have come about, however, until she decided for herself that she would not be crippled if she should be hit or that she could certainly take that much pain since she clearly could see she had done it countless times before.

Her mother was curious as to how I was able to settle Mary down and rid her of the fear especially when Mary would simply sit and listen.

"She told me when we left here that she hardly said anything to you but that you did all the talking. I've tried that at home and when she becomes stubborn and won't answer me I get angry because I think I'm wasting my time."

"Lots of parents think so," I replied to Mary's mother. "The truth of the matter is that most kids are listening to their parents but just because they don't want to answer them is no sign that the adult is not getting through. When you want to instruct Mary again, and she becomes quiet, keep making your point over and over again, using different logical arguments each time until she sees it. Some kids require lots of persuasion and will weigh each of your arguments. This takes time and they should be allowed to have it, days, if necessary. Kids respect good, sound, logical reasoning, even if they disagree with you openly. Keep up the logic and the reasoning and you can often get them to see common sense if you give them a little time."

I received a nice letter one day from Mary after the vacation started, saying that she was promoted and glad to be out of that class and grateful for my help in getting her through.

That a physical pain need not lead to or be the cause of an

emotional pain is not widely recognized although it has been widely observed. A child may laugh with delight in getting ten swats on the seat of his pants on his birthday, yet he may cry upon getting only one from his angry father for not getting ready for bed. A pain is a pain and we cannot do much about our injuries at times. However, whether we become emotionally upset over our physical aches depends a great deal on our rational thinking. By thinking clearly over our physical illnesses or injuries, we do not intensify that pain and must put up only with *it*. If, however, we become alarmed, fearful, or angry over our physical pains we then must wrestle with two pains, one caused by the outside and physical in nature, the other caused by our irrational thoughts and mental in nature.

All children should be taught to deal calmly with their cuts, bruises, or illnesses. If a finger is cut, while it is being bandaged, the child must be encouraged to think calmly by pointing out the uselessness of his fears, the realization that it will pain for only a short while, and that in two days he will probably be able to remove the bandage.

For such illnesses as hay fever, ulcers, a physical deformity, etc., which do in fact restrict the child's activities for days, weeks, or even years, the parent must be careful not to agree with the child that these illnesses in and of themselves are causing his misery. What is true is the fact that such a child's life is filled with more frustration than another's. We have seen over and over again how it is not one's frustrations which cause our emotional misery, rather it is our attiudes toward these frustrations.

The mother or father who is constantly making allowances for his or her child so that it is not required to do chores, learn discipline, learn neatness or perseverance, because the child is blind, crippled, or sick at certain times of the year is doing that child no favor. Instead of learning to make the most of his affliction such a child will go through life expecting everyone to make an exception just for him and to allow him to justify his unhappiness because of his illness. This may sound unfeeling, but it is not. It is sensible and very considerate. The child with some malady or handicap needs less self-pity than more normal children since he has higher hurdles to jump. If his frustrations are greater he should be better trained to deal with them. Being overly sentimental about them only increases the child's weakness rather than decreases it. Remember, therefore, a physical hurt causes genuine physical pain. Any emotoinal pain which accompanies this pain is needless and if carefully challenged can be eliminated.

CHAPTER VIII

Fear of Rejection and Ridicule

Just this past week I had three grade-school children referred to me because they were either not living up to their potential, they were getting into endless petty difficulties, or they disliked school so much it was a battle each day to make them go to school.

As so often happens upon looking deeper into these problems they all had one complaint in common: other children did not like them and they were being called names. Without exception each child reacted in such a manner as to make his situation worse, not better. Becoming angry over the name-calling only lead to more baiting, and this anger when directed against the offenders made them more distant and rejecting. Both of these reactions are then assessed by the victim children who become more disturbed and this in turn brings on greater name-calling and further rejection. This cycle can go to such lengths that a child who gets caught on this merry-go-round finds himself eventually so disliked and picked on that he becomes delinquent, lonely, and probably also depressed.

It is a pity because this difficulty is not really a great difficulty at all. In every case of name-calling, brought to my attention I have so far been able to bring around its termination almost completely in no more than four weeks. A parent or teacher who finds a child troubled in this fashion would do well to remember (by heart if necessary) some of the following logical arguments I have used in these cases.

I will usually start out my conversation with the child by asking what names he is being called. If he is too embarrassed to tell me, I make up one I think might apply. Thus a stout child I assume might be called "Fatso," a small child, "Runt," etc. In any event this is not important, only helpful. What is important is teachnig the child that names can never hurt him, that he is getting himself upset, and that if he wants the name-calling to stop he must learn to ignore it.

Bill, an eleven-year-old, cried frequently while telling me how unpopular he was. He would not say what he was being called so I tried to attack his problem in a general way.

"So they call you names. Why do you take them seriously?"

"I don't like it. They're mean to me and the things they call me hurt very much."

"No they don't Billy. Nothing they *say* can ever hurt you. Even if they called you nasty names all day it couldn't upset you unless you let it. You're the one who's hurting you, not them. The only real way they can ever hurt you is if they punch you, or push you, break your bones, cut your skin, or make you bleed. But this usually doesn't happen does it?"

"No. But sometimes I get into fights with them and then I may get hurt."

"Right, and then their blows will actually be hurting you. And if you didn't listen to their nonsense the situation probably wouldn't get out of hand to the point where you're getting beat up. I'd like to show you how to handle this sort of thing so they'll probably stop. But even if they don't stop you need never be upset by what pecple say to you."

"But words can hurt me." he insisted.

"No they can't. Words are nothing but air from the throat that's set vibrating. It moves through the air like a ripple in a pond when you throw in a rock. Then it reaches your ears. That kind of moving air cannot hurt you. What does upset you is what you're telling yourself at the same time that they're calling you names. That can hurt plenty. If you think to yourself that it's awful to be called names, or be disliked or that you're no good because they don't like you, then it's these thoughts of your own rather than their words which upset you."

"What can I do?"

"Keep thinking clearly about it and you can never upset yourself. Tell yourself over and over things like: 'Sticks and stones can break my bones but names can never harm me.' Then tell yourself that *they've* got a problem and if they want to be angry at you or think mean things of you, that's their right, even if they are wrong in what they think."

"I don't understand that."

"Well, if they accuse you of stinking let's say, they're either right or they're wrong, aren't they? And if they are right admit it since its true and try hard not to stink anymore. And be grateful someone pointed it out to you because you wouldn't want to go around smelling all the time would you, if you could help it?"

"No."

"And if what they're saying is false ignore it if you can't calmly show them they're wrong. It's their opinion, and right or wrong they have a right to an opinion different from yours. So just tell yourself they're not perfect and in this they're especially mistaken. So they've got a problem. Poor kids."

"But what if they still call me names?"

"They won't if you stop reacting to them. Everytime you get mad or hurt over their name-calling they have a good time and the next time they're looking for fun they'll say to themselves, 'Let's go and call Billy names. He always gets mad and cries. He's lots of fun.' But if you don't get mad and cry they'll get tired of the whole business after a time and probably stop it." Then at this point I usually use the following illustration:

"Have you ever gone fishing Billy?"

"Yes."

"Well when you throw your line in and don't get any nibbles what do you do?"

"Try again I suppose."

"And after trying a few times what do you do then?"

"Try some place else or go home."

"Fine. Now that's what any sensible person would do. And that's what these fellows are doing with you each day during recess or after school. They want to have fun and their fun is just like going fishing. They say to themselves, 'We had good fishing so far with Billy, let's go after him again.' Then they throw out their bait which is their name calling. And lo and behold what does the fish Billy do?"

"He takes the bait," Billy said with an embarrassed smile.

"Right. And they keep saying to themselves that the fishing is real good today so let's come back to do this tomorrow. And of course they're right. They're hoping you'll get upset and you do. Now what do you suppose they'd do if you didn't take their bait?"

"They'd probably keep it up for a while but if I didn't let it bother me they'd go fishing some place else."

"Bravo. Do you suppose you could do that?"

"I'll try, but how can I be sure I won't get mad even though I know it won't do me any good?"

"By reminding yourself over and over of several things. First, keep saying to yourself, 'Sticks and stones will break my bones but names will never hurt me.' Secondly, tell yourself that they have a problem, and you don't have to be disturbed just because they're kooky and enjoy seeing others cry. And thirdly, let it in one ear and out the other by just not caring too much whether they like you or not. Remember, its not going to kill you if they don't like you too much. Take it easy, be nice to them in return and in time they'll probably change their attitudes."

This technique has worked remarkably well, both in terms of effectively ridding the child of being called names, and in terms of the time required to do so. A few weeks usually stops the whole procedure.

The fear of rejection is perhaps more frequent among conforming adolescents. To be popular is one of the most important goals of that age span. Not infrequently it spills over into adulthood where it can cause just as much misery as it does with the children.

Rejection is a natural behavior of people. It is simply not possible to be accepted and liked all the time by everyone. Therefore, rejection by someone, sometimes is inevitable. This fact, if realized, would reduce the sufferings of a great many people. But they instead feel falsely they must be liked by almost everyone especially the people they themselves like, and unless this is fulfilled a catastrophe has happened.

A parent should show his child that there is a difference between wanting to be liked and having to be liked. When the child is disturbed about not being included in the clique the child should be reminded forcefully that no one is perfect and can satisfy all needs at one time; that his rejection tells us something about the persons doing the rejection but says nothing about the rejected person; and that as long as the rejection is not so complete that one is unable to buy food or clothing, it is not really a catastrophe, only a regrettable frustration and annoyance.

The adult is certainly free to use his own logical arguments to help his child over being disturbed because of rejection, but for what it is worth I present some which I have had good success with.

A fourteen-year-old girl complained bitterly through tears

and depression that her mother did not love her.

"So why get upset?"

"How would you feel if your wife didn't love you?"

"I wouldn't like it, but I wouldn't be upset."

"You wouldn't? Then you couldn't love her very much."

"On the contrary. I do. But if she didn't love me I'd have to get on the ball and do what I calmly could to get her to change her attitude. And if it's true that your mother doesn't love you, instead of getting upset and angry with her as you've been doing, what have you done so she might love you more?"

"Why should I do anything? She's the one who's rejecting me, not me her?"

"Because you're complaining about not being loved, she isn't. You've got the problem. Why should she do anything about your problem if you won't?"

"What *can* I do?"

"First, not get upset. How? By not taking her rejection of you in a personal way. You probably think that if mother doesn't love you it must be because you're a bad girl and are no good."

"Yes I do feel that."

"Prove that statement, that if someone doesn't like you it proves you're no good."

"Why else would they dislike you?"

"For reasons of their own. Maybe she's immature and doesn't know how to be patient with kids. Maybe she's jealous of your youth and wishes she too could play hop-scotch. I really don't know. But the point I'm getting at is she could dislike you for any number of reasons, none of which have to do with you personally. You however, take each rejection personally."

"I still don't see why her rejecting me doesn't prove I'm no good."

'Okay, if your mother went shopping for fruit and selected

lemons, grapefruits, and peaches but did not buy apples, what does that prove?"

"That she doesn't like apples."

"Why doesn't it prove apples are bad? That's what you've been telling me?"

"Oh but that's different."

Of course it was not different and I simply continued to insist that if a rejection of apples was not a reflection of apples why should a rejection of her be a reflection of her own worthwhileness.

Finally after some weeks she was able to say, "I'm beginning to get your point. I can be rejected by my mother because she's human and has tastes about people just like she has for clothes, and that if she doesn't always love me I suddenly don't become something I wasn't before, but remain the same."

"Certainly. You've become less important to her, but not less important to yourself. You only become disturbed when you are no longer important to you. That thought can hurt. The other cannot."

Rejection among one's friends is very common. Fortunately our children do not make too much of this since broken friendships are often repaired within minutes or at most a few days. A few children take rejection so hard and so personally they fight their friends, call them names, withdraw, or get others to change their feelings against the aforementioned. All these tactics usually bring on more rejection which encourages the child to fight harder which brings on more rejection, etc. until the child is truly upset and a lone wolf. And if he were told he brought 90% of this sorry state upon his head all by himself, would he believe it? Hardly, but to help him he must eventually come to see that he was his own worst enemy.

Take the case of David, thirteen years of age, who was reasonably bright but was failing in school in addition to causing numerous disturbances. He felt unaccepted, which was by now quite true, and his resentment over being ignored propelled him into striking out at smaller children, and cursing at the older ones. Finally his rebellion reached the point where he could not relate to anyone in a friendly way, but was instantly on the defensive lest he be hurt. He pushed, punched (all in a joking way) to establish a relationship. Children did not take to this and showed their annoyance. He was ready for this and soon found himself fighting the very person he wanted to befriend.

"Why don't you treat them nicely David, if you want them to be nice to you?"

"Because they're not nice to me." he said trying to hold back tears.

"But why get mad at people just because they're not nice to you?"

"Aren't people supposed to be nice to each other?"

"No, who says so?"

"The Bible says love thy neighbor."

"That's wonderful advice, but does it mean everyone must accept advice just because it's wonderful?"

"No I guess not. But it would be better if they did."

"Of course it would. And if everyone was a perfect saint we'd all realize that and take good advice. Do you know anyone with a halo around his head?"

"No."

"Well, if people can't be saints you must expect them to do unsaintly things, such as turn down good advice. Even more important however, if you dislike their behavior so much why do you turn around and do the same thing? Isn't it wrong when you treat them unkindly, if its wrong when they treat you unkindly? What's good for the goose is good for the gander. Your problem is that you insist all people should be perfect and that's impossible. That's why you get so upset all the time. If you wouldn't take them so seriously, and try to be nicer when they don't like you, sooner or later they might get to like you very much."

In time he tried being nicer and this immediately took the sting out of the other children. They could hardly continue being indifferent to someone who was making every effort to be nice despite their attempts at making him miserable. Soon he had more friends, was being included in the gang, and felt wanted. He occasionally had a slip but had learned his lesson well enough to recover and repair the damage before it got out of hand.

Special Reminders About Fears

1. Do not proceed too fast in helping a child desensitize himself to fears. If the pressure is too great, he will not only keep his original fear, but develop a fear of the adult who is recklessly pushing him into the "dangerous" activity. Gradual gains are more impressive in the long run, because they tend to take hold. In practice, it will be found that this slow period is not as long as it would seem at first. The pace of recovery is frequently slow at first, but quickly picks up speed.

2. Praise and encouragement are essential and should be supplied in liberal doses. Failures should be taken as a matter of fact, without discouragement. Support from an adult is vital at the time of a failure as it is at no other period of the learning process. Success is its own reward, but failure, left solely to the child to deal with, can easily reverse an otherwise potential success.

3. Imitation is still one of the easiest ways children learn attitudes and philosophies. When a child reacts with fear, he is proving he has learned society's lessons all too well. All supervisors should set the best examples they can. Does the teacher become morose because the class play was mediocre? Her students can observe this and unwittingly accept this as normal and natural. The camp counselor who himself fears rejection

by the other counselors can be of pitifully little assistance to the boy who is struggling for acceptance by his peers.

4. Overcoming the fear of failure ought to be given more attention in the school. Class discussions, prepared lectures and personal annecdote could play a vital role towards getting the students to question seriously how catastrophic it really is to fail occasionally.

Most important of all, teachers and parents must be careful not to become intellectual fascists. This is the notion that those people are superior who have superior intellects. There are all kinds of fascisms of which this is probably one of the more common varieties. It is fascistic to think one group superior to commoners because it has royal blood, that Aryans are superior to Jews, that white-skinned people are better than black-skinned, or that smart people are better than dull ones. The error is always the same: one class is supposedly superior to another because it possesses qualities which are then highly esteemed. In another time or place, these values could change completely. As long as children today see the value we put on intelligence, they are likely to feel inferior, not only as intellects (which would be sound) but inferior as persons (which would be absurd). Each child has a right in the universe, and there is a place for each.

5. Especially for those children fearful of ridicule and rejection, it is important that the counselor of the moment cast doubt on those rejecting persons for the child. He can only feel crushed by rejection if he values the rejecter too highly. This over-esteem must be undermind. Even the child's parents can be cast in a more realistic light for the child without its losing respect for them. The inquiry can always be raised why it is that everyone else is such an expert, but never the child in question, or how can they, as imperfect people, always be correct and the child always wrong? This sounds perhaps like a dangerous undermining of all authority figures. In fact,

it is a healthy, sobering appraisal of the fallible mortals the child deals with. From this can come true respect, possible only after fear of authority figures has been diminished.

6. Homework is vital to overcoming any fear. Rather than allow the child to avoid the feared activity and thereby learn less about it, he should be encouraged to become increasingly familiar with the fear. Fear of swimming can not easily be reduced by the child who never takes another step in the water. He must be made to return to the scene of his fears and urged by slow steps to acquaint himself with this dreaded task. A planned program, outlining in some detail what is expected each week, and geared so moderately as to insure some success, can do wonders.

7. Reason is a powerful weapon against all fears, but unless the reasoning is clear and at the level of the child's comprehension, it will go over his head. Simple examples, therefore, can serve to make deeper philosophical issues quite clear. Most adults can, with a bit of forethought, construct such examples. The more the better; the simpler the better.

8. Do not be too eager to remove the fearful situations or objects such as potentially harmful toys, a neurotic teacher, or a rejecting friend. Such is the stuff of which life is made, and the child who has them removed loses the opportunity to learn how to deal with them. Some feared and dangerous objects will, of course, have to be removed such as a large dog around a small child. But this is too often being done by the too well-meaning parent. It is far better that he learn to overcome his neurotic thinking than to expect the world to shape itself around his desires.

9. A child is not born with fears despite what the old wives tales tell us. Fears are learned and can therefore be unlearned. All of us have done precisely this during our lives, and need but reflect one moment over our childhoods to realize the large numbers of fears we have mastered since then.

10. The superstitious notions most commonly related to fears are the following: (1) We must be loved; (2) To be acceptable to oneself, one must be totally competent; (3) It is horrible if some things do not go our way; (4) Others can cause our unhappiness; (5) Worrying is unavoidable and makes good sense; (6) We cannot help becoming upset over other people's problems.

CHAPTER IX

Anger

If adults knew nothing else about children but how to control their anger, this contribution would make an immense difference in the world. A new generation of adults, free of this hostile habit could make peace a universal reality. So long, however, as we are ourselves so poorly schooled in the psychology of hate we cannot expect people to deal with one another in a spirit of love.

Rational counseling maintains that man has as much control over his angers and resentments as he has over his other negative emotions. Properly instructed, it is perfectly possible to raise children who will not get angry over most normally provoking situations. Regrettably, that day is still far in the future, but the means of achieving it exist now. I do not regard this as far-fetched since my own practice has given me abundant evidence of the frequency with which some of the worst cases of anger can change if they are properly instructed. Not that these children were made humorless or colorless because they capped their stormy reactions. No indeed. What did happen was that they became more colorful and relaxed, more sensible in their dealings with others and thus they were treated better by them in turn. Their lives became happy rather than periodically stormy. And, not being torn apart with these violent internal forces they could give full attention to their budding creative skills.

But most children, and adults too, for that matter, have a fear of losing their angry ways. It is the sword and shield by which they protect themselves from an attacking and frustrating world. To give up such defensive equipment is tantamount in their minds to surrender. Rather than accept domination they prefer anger.

If it were truly a choice between being used by others and suffering occasional high blood pressure there would be no quarrel. Even anger, with all its companion distresses of loss of appetite, loss of sleep, stomach cramps, headaches, etc., would be worth it if it would really free us from these assaults. Often, however, it does not reduce the neurotic behavior around us. Instead it tends to create more of it. When it does work, the price of waging the war and bearing the burden of anger is too high.

Anger is equated with firmness in the minds of most children and adults. "No one is going to push me around," they heatedly insist. Their assumption is always that to be firm and stand one's ground one must also growl over it like a dog with a bone. The idea that one can be as solid as the Rock of Gibraltar and as peaceful as a sunny day, both at the same time is absolutely foreign to the angry child. Yet such is the lesson he will have to learn if he is to have a peaceful life and if this is ever to be a peaceful world.

The dynamics of anger are surprisingly simple. The baby gets mad when it does not get what it demands. Anyone else who shows anger does precisely the same thing. The wish, desire, or preference, which is harmless and can only lead to disappointment if frustrated is converted into a need, necessity, or demand. Should these be frustrated the emotional reaction is intense anger, resentment, and bitterness.

The victim of these emotional states must be taught never

to think in such extreme terms. His belief that someone, or something *must* comply with him has to be questioned until he relinquishes his demand. This will guarantee him a degree of mental peace which he can use to gain his ends in a more controlled fashion.

I have had a number of very bright students referred to me by school counselors who complained that these adolescents were clearly not working up to their great potential. A composite of such a case in point was Richard Quest. For years he had been sullen and defiant at school, earned mediocre grades, and since entering high school was especially rebellious. He did extremely well only in those subjects he liked or with teachers he personally found equal to his intellectual caliber. Outside of school the same disdain for the average person prevailed. It was his teachers, however, for whom he reserved his choicest words.

"You'd think those blockheads would appreciate the fact that it becomes unnecessary to do twenty math problems when the principle of their solution is grasped after doing two. But no, they give you an F if you don't do the whole assignment even if it can't teach you something further. And then there are those cute reports they ask for on experiments or books we've read. First you make a ridiculous outline, then draw up a first draft, and finally hand in a finished paper. If one has the ability to do this piddling work in one operation, do you think they accept that? No sir! I get an F for my paper because I didn't go through the intermediate steps. How assinine can people be?" He was by now quite red-faced and composureless.

He continued, "I obviously can't go along with these dopes so I'm determined to make them change to more sensible ways. Whenever I can, I show up the teacher before the class. You'd be amazed at how often they misquote books and authors."

This was his plan of attack: humiliate the people who were frustrating him in the hope of showing them how wrong and stupid their unfair teaching practices were. The harder he tried the ruder he became until his rebellion blossomed into visible contempt.

I began, "Look Dick, you keep giving me this song and dance about how stupid other people are. Okay, so they're stupid. If that's the way they are, that's the way they are. Why spoil all your precious years in high school over someone else's problems? I admire your attempt to change them but if you're so smart why do you keep doing the same thing which experience has taught you doesn't work?"

"Such as?" he asked sarcastically.

"Such as rebelling and humiliating them. If this worked I'd say, 'Bravo, go ahead with more of the same!' But how successful has this plan of yours been? How many teachers have you succeeded into admitting they were stupid? How many have dropped their irritating teaching practices?"

"None I'm afraid."

"So upon your own admission you've had no success with your strategy of sarcasm, humiliation, and rebellion. If it didn't work yesterday, and hasn't worked in the past two years, isn't it about time to recognize your method of solving this problem stinks and you'd better think of something else? You keep flaunting your own intelligence in front of others, yet you act blindly and stupidly yourself."

"Stupidly? For trying to get them to be more adult and sensible?"

"No. For pigheadedly insisting they have to change their ways."

"But their teaching practices are atrocious."

"That's their problem, not yours."

"I'm the one that suffers under them though."

"I'd hardly say you suffered *because* of them. You may be annoyed, all right, but suffer, no. Any suffering you've gone through has been created by you, just plain ole little you."

"By me? How do you figure that."

"Because you know they have authority over you and are not going to accept insults from a student by just lying down. But that doesn't slow you down one bit. You keep up your attack and they, rightly or wrongly, lash out at you with the few weapons they have, such as keeping you after school, giving irritating homework assignments, and most serious of all, giving you poor grades. And don't tell me you aren't suffering because of that?"

"Yes, I confess you're right on that score. I seriously question if I'll be able to get into one of those private eastern schools I've been counting on."

"There, you see how you compounded your dilemma?"

Dick needed a few moments to let this sink in. His righteous wrath was so strong he could not quickly look at the vital part *he* was playing in his troubles. He, like many youngsters who feel they are absolutely correct over the issue in question, ignore the fact that they may be right on the issue but totally inefficient over handling it. For this reason I was not attacking him on his stand against his teachers. Whether I agreed or not it would not, at this time, have mattered. What was essential to get him to see was the totally self-damaging way he was going about righting these supposed wrongs.

He resumed the discussion, this time a bit more attentive to what I had to offer.

"How would you have handled this?"

"By keeping my mouth shut after I could see I wasn't getting anywhere, and doing what was expected of me. Then after graduating with high honors I'd have gone to the best school and gotten my Ph.D. in education. Then I would have written my heart out in books, speeches, and articles until my views had some influence. At the same time I would have run for my local school board and tried to implement better practices right then and there."

Here I was demonstrating to Dick two ideas: first, not all

problems can be solved when we want them solved. and second, there is more than one way to skin a cat.

Bright as he was he could not yet see this and resumed his attack.

"Why should I have to put up with their idiotic ways now? They're repulsive."

"Why shouldn't you have to put up with them?" I answered firmly but calmly. "You want your high school diploma and they're calling the shots. If you don't like their rules, you're always free to quit the game."

"Now doctor, you know very well I'm not going to be a drop-out. It's unthinkable."

"I quite agree. It would be senseless. And it's just for that reason you *should* put up with their imperfect methods. Unless you do you won't reach your goals. What better reason can you think of for going along with them? Incidentally, you're also acting like a dunce about another matter."

"What's that?"

"You keep telling yourself after each one of these frustrations that they can't do this or they can't do that when in reality the thing has already *been* done."

This is where we had our first laugh.

"Is this what you psychologists call reality testing?" He asked.

"Yes, something like that. If you wanted to go swimming but the water was cold you wouldn't say it shouldn't be cold, would you? Nature could care less whether you approved or not. If you want to swim badly enough you're better off accepting it and making the most of it rather than acting neurotic about it.

"Your problem," I summarized, "is that you insist on having everything your way, especially when you're right."

"But holy smokes, when I *am* right I *should* have my way."

"Who says so? Richard Quest, that's who. Your teachers

don't think you're right, and if they truly believe you're wrong, shouldn't they make you conform to their practices?"

"That's just it Doctor Hauck. You know and I know their methods are superficial and outdated. Doesn't being right have any bearing over the matter?"

"Only on the issue of *who* is right or wrong, not over the issue of whether people have to *do* the right thing. People by the very fact that they are human and imperfect have a right to be wrong. You are dictatorially refusing them the right to be imperfect. Are you God?"

He thought about this a while and answered, "In other words, you don't disagree with my complaints about my teachers but only the fact that because they and I disagree, they must adopt my views."

"Agreed. I sympathize with your frustrations completely. You are asked to do needless tasks which they, because of their rigidity and shortsightedness, will not lift. There's no reason for saying they can't do these things since they're wrong, because people aren't faultless and are expected to do silly, pointless things. But this is no reason why the whole world should straighten itself out to please you or prevent you from angrily sabotaging yourself. Now what do you suppose you'll have to do about all this?"

"Shudder the thought. I'll have to conform. As you say they're in charge and if I don't want to cut my nose to spite my face I'll have to go along with them, like it or not."

"And precisely which irrational idea will you have to challenge each time you become defiant?"

"Let's see now. That it's awful not to get my way and that if they have problems I should get upset over them. Is that right?"

"Amen Dick."

It was a long, hard struggle getting this brilliant boy to accept reality and its demands. Neurosis has no fear of intelligence. This boy was using his ability to hurt himself in the same neurotic way a duller child might have. As Doctor Ellis has so nicely pointed out. "A neurotic is a non-stupid person who behaves stupidly."

In time Dick learned not to blame his less gifted teachers and accepted his lot philosophically. He quickly jumped in grades and was easily able to enter a fine university. In his final session he said, "This has been a tremendous philosophical experience for me. Accepting people as they are has helped immensely. I can no longer get smolderingly disturbed over their shortcomings. I wish they were different to be sure, but they aren't. I'm going to have to live with these kinds of persons since most of the world falls in their group. And if I just stop demanding I must have my way because I am right I'm sure I'll be much less disturbed over their foibles. Then I can calmly try to improve them or just let the whole thing go for the present until I can influence them."

Reasoning and sound logic won the day and turned a potential delinquent into a socially responsible citizen. He was benefited mostly by differentiating a frustration from a disturbance. Never during the time required for our sessions, or during the rest of his time in high school was his frustration changed even a little. Yet his disturbance went the gamut from intense resentment which was causing him the greatest possible harm to his future career, to an accepting, friendly, unnoticeable irritation.

All anger is righteous to those having it. Some anger is so easily comprehended by others it becomes accepted as just and therefore socially righteous. This is the most difficult kind to modify.

Thomas Hayle's best friend once made a very unpleasant remark about Tom's sister. So infuriated was he that he leaped at his buddy and proceeded to trounce him with all his might. Two teachers were needed to remove him from the injured boy. Although Tom was temporarily expelled from school public sympathy was on his side. It was not guilt therefore, which drove him to me but his fear of his own anger. He had come dangerously close to homicide and knew it.

"You've got to help me control my temper, Doc. Before I know it I can get furious and I'm always sorry for it afterwards even though I figure the guy has it coming."

"What are you sorry about in that case?"

"Because I overdo it. Once I get a little mad I get all mad."

Here was a unique plea. A boy wanted to erase his temper while believing it was legitimate.

"Sounds like you want me to teach you how to get to take drugs without becoming addicted. It's no good, Tom. Either you decide to make war on anger completely or forget it. No matter how you figure it out, anger is wrong morally and dangerous to yourself and others."

"But doctor, everybody gets angry."

"And everyone gets cavities. What does that prove? Only that anger is a regrettable burden man must constantly fight or he'll destroy himself."

"Gee doctor, you talk like a fellow should never get angry, even when he has a right to it."

"You never have a *legitimate* right to get mad although you have a perfect *neurotic* right to that any time you want it."

He looked puzzled. "I know what you're thinking, Tom, that you had a perfect right to beat up on your former friend for the nasty things he said."

"That's right. And I did too!"

"No, you didn't. You almost hurt that kid pretty badly merely because he said something you didn't approve of."

"Well, what more reason did I need?"

"Only if he had attacked you physically would you be morally correct in using violence. As it was he merely shot off his mouth, something he has a perfect right to."

"A perfect right to call my sister a pig?" he demanded.

"Certainly, why not? You didnt' have to take it as an insult.

That was your choice. And make no mistake about it you did have a choice."

"All right, suppose that guy had called my mother something awful. That would make a difference wouldn't it?" he asked rhetorically.

"No. That's still his right. Look at it this way, Tom. Either he's right and your sister is a pig or she isn't. All you need to do to avoid getting angry is to ask yourself this question each time an accusation is made and you'll still be undisturbed."

"Even if it's wrong?"

"Sure. Analyze it this way. Ask yourself quite honestly if your sister is a pig. If she's fat and sloppy and smacks when she eats then maybe the accusation has some truth to it. Then you could thank your friend for pointing this out to you and decide what you want to do about your sister so she doesn't act like a pig. There's really no good reason to get sore at him since in that case he would have been telling the truth.

"But suppose you decide he's wrong, that your sister is a very presentable person who is not offensive to others. Still no reason to get furious. Simply remind youself that it's his opinion against yours and that if he can be so wrong he must be pretty disturbed. You might even sympathize for the poor guy for being such a nut. Now you can hardly get too shook up if you look at it this way can you?"

Tom had to admit it sounded sensible but I knew this point would have to be reviewed a number of times before he could accept it. His next remark showed a misunderstanding which many people have on first learning of these principles.

"So I should never do anything to fellows when they're mean. Just keep myself from getting mad?"

"I didn't say that, Tom. All I've told you how to do is not get emotionally disturbed. We haven't talked about handling the frustrations at all."

I proceeded to show Tom that he could and indeed should

do his best to stop being treated unfairly by others. If he did nothing they would only tend to be more mean. However, if he got angry each time he was frustrated by someone then his only solution would likely be some form of physical violence. This is often totally uncalled for because much better solutions are available. He could, for instance, have asked his friend what was really on his mind that he would make such an unkind remark. By showing his continued friendship and understanding his buddy might have retracted his hasty statement. Should this tactic fail he could take the matter to his teachers who might have a talk with the boy. And if such talk became really serious both sets of parents could be called in to settle the issue. Actual libel, of course can always be turned over to an attorney.

"So you see Tom, there are a number of possibilities you might have resorted to had you had a clear enough head to think them out. And anyone of them would have been employed without the slightest bit of anger. As it stands you've managed to hurt him, almost seriously and what's equally regrettable is the fact that you haven't gotten him to think better of your sister either, have you?"

"I'm afraid not. Now he hates me too."

"There you go. Now he's probably thinking that you're a skunk and that sis is still a pig. Some progress isn't it!"

Special Reminders about Anger

1. No matter what the reason, anger is neurotic, not legitimate. It is a purely childish demand that life must conform to us. Even when our demands are altruistic, "You must stop drinking" we are still neurotically insisting we must have our way. The two sentences immediately preceding this emotion are: 1) I want, wish, or desire something (a harmless thought which can only lead to mild frustration and disappointment; and 2) therefore, I must have that something (a sick thought

which leads to hatred even though the frustration is the same as it was for the wish).

2. An angry child should always be reminded that he will more easily right a wrong or get his way in the end if he avoids this intense emotion. The feeling of anger plus doing something about the frustration often succeed it is true. But so does the doing itself! The hate is an unnecessary burden and can well be disposed of.

If physical force seems required, this too can be employed calmly as every boxer knows. Parents in fact quite frequently spank their children while remaining reasonably unperturbed themselves. The squelching of anger is not a plea for surrender. The trouble is that anger and getting things done are so frequently witnessed following one another we have wrongly been led to believe they are inseparable.

3. Older theories of emotions held that anger should not be pent up inside ourselves. In this repressed state it causes real internal damage such as high blood pressure. For this reason the public has long been advised to "ventilate hostile feelings."

There is some credence to this assertion. All of us have felt better after "blowing off steam," or working off our fury with the punching bag.

But how much better it is not to create these hostile feelings in the first place! By reasoning soundly we prevent our frustrations from getting to the point where anger is created and then drained off.

4. In teaching children to control hostility, one of the adults' most persuasive arguments, is pointing out the harm the child himself sustains when he seeks revenge. The damage to his peace of mind and his physical system is considerable. He should be shown that what his enemy started, he is finishing. For he, the hater, is usually treating himself far more mercilessly than the frustrator is. Were the other fellow really causing him such mental anguish the child would scream his head off.

When *he* whips himself into a fury and suffers more from this than the original frustration he makes no effort to stop it. In fact, he gets angrier at the other fellow for "giving" him this anger. Hate cannot be given with impunity. If a child wishes to smash another child over the head with a cactus, he too will suffer pain.

5. Typical irrational notions behind anger are: 3) some people are wicked and need severe punishment to correct this; 4) things have to go our way; 5) emotional stress is created by the environment; and 10) we should become disturbed over other people's behavior.

CHAPTER X

Worry and Depression

It is as difficult for a child to remain unworried over a crisis as it is for adults. Of all the irrational emotions, such as anger or fear, none are quite the same as anxiety or depression. They are frequent companions to one another and often difficult to relieve. Worry has in common with depression the tendency to remain active once set in motion. While anger is usually short-lived, and fear can be reduced by avoiding the feared situation, depression and worry are like glue. Only the most diligent application can undo the web these twin monsters spin over their victims. Indeed, they often appear together in the same person during the same crisis and seem to be one phenomenon, not two.

The superstition which creates worry is the belief that if something dreadful can happen the utmost concern should be given the event and it should never be allowed to lose our attention. Not only do children believe worry is unavoidable, but that the crisis cannot resolve itself properly unless it is constantly brooded over. It is as though the excessive focusing had some power to prevent the dangerous or awful event.

These dynamics were crystal clear in the case of 13-year-old Billy who was referred by both his priest and doctor. The boy was preoccupied with the thought his mother would die and leave him hopelessly abandoned. Neither the clergyman's assurances nor the physician's tranquilizers were sufficient to quiet his nerves.

His priest consulted me and used our talks to great advantage. It seemed Billy was very keenly aware of anything relating to death and his mother's health. He knew precisely the number of deaths in the community each week, when a funeral was scheduled, even where the local undertaker was most of the time. His mind was never far off this morbid subject.

To assist the counselor it was necessary to get him to change his approach from one of mere sympathy and support, to one of reasoning. In such cases the child must learn to look at two questions very seriously. Firstly, was his mother really in danger, and, secondly, did he have to think of nothing but her health? Unless both ideas were repeatedly debated, he would not find the peace he was looking for.

The priest helped Billy with the first question by asking him to talk with his mother and her doctor about her health. He was assigned reading to inform him what had been done to her. The more one knows of a subject the less fear he has of it.

Armed with that, however, it was still necessary to show Billy how to talk himself into using it as a weapon against this worry. Each time he had the thought his mother might get sick again he was to use this information to cancel out this belief.

At the same time the idea that he should worry over her had to be attacked and completely dispelled. Arguments were presented to him, such as: his worring could do absolutely nothing against another disease; someday his mother would die despite all his efforts; his worrying and depression were already making life about as miserable for him as her death itself would. When these sallies proved insufficient he was reminded of the worry his worrying was indirectly creating for his mother.

The guardian of such a child can think of numerous logical rebuttals and should expose the child to each of them, countering each objection forcefully and convincingly. If necessary, he should have explained to him the workings of the mind so he can understand his mental habit from a theoretical viewpoint. Some time should be taken to explain how the subject is literally creating his own worry and that his mother's life or death has relatively little to do with it. We *can* control our thoughts. They do not control us. Billy, through the urging of his minister, was advised to focus on neutral or happy thoughts. He was to stop scanning the obituary column and to resist noticing each car on the street to see if it was the mortician's.

His priest informed me he had already covered some of this ground with Billy but to little avail.

"Then apparently he is still not convinced he is making himself concentrate on death."

"Yes," he replied, "I'm sure he still believes the thought springs from nowhere and he is a helpless victim of it."

"And how did you respond to that?"

"I'm afraid I fumbled a bit because I didn't know how to proceed."

"You might have shown the boy how he is not bothered by other thoughts which are equally true but which he is not even spending a second's worry on."

"He is?"

"Certainly he is. Everytime he gets into a car these days he has a pretty good chance of being crippled or killed in an accident doesn't he? That's a pretty awful thing to happen to him but he doesn't even notice it. If all awful thoughts can involuntarily plague our minds, why isn't that one?"

In this fashion the problem was somewhat reduced. His counselor felt, however, something else needed to be done to finish the job, something new perhaps.

"Have you been asking Billy to train himself to identify his thoughts whenever he becomes nervous and depressed? A clue can usually be found there if the person is training himself to be more conscious of his thinking."

"You mean," the priest inquired, "Have I detected all his irrational ideas at point B? I can think of one theme he keeps bringing up but I'm not sure it's unreasonable."

"What's that?"

"He'll be all alone with no one to care for him if she dies."

"That's irrational isn't it?" I asserted.

"True, for I'm sure his grandmother or aunt would be willing to take him in. I confess though the thought of losing his mother does seem catastrophic to me too and therefore his fear *is* reasonable."

Now I began to see why Billy had not recovered faster. Unless his counselor is completely convinced that Billy is wrong in his beliefs, the boy will reuse this doubt and make an agreement of it. A thorough challenging of his neurotic beliefs is not possible under these circumstances. For a time our attention was placed on the instructor rather than the child until he himself was firmly convinced of several things: 1. Billy's mother was in no immediate danger; 2. even if she were the boy's worrying over this catastrophe would be pointless and only bring on *further* misery to himself; 3. that he could avoid these alarming thoughts if he worked very hard to convince himself of this truth; and 4. that life would be saddened by her illness or death to be sure but it would not end or be hopelessly unhappy for the rest of his life. Thus renewed the priest was able to be more convincing and over a period of weekly sessions for four months was able to bring calm back into Billy's life.

We have said that nervousness and depression often go together. A good example of such a case was that of Linda, a nine-year-old who had the thought one day she might kill her six-year-old brother. It first occurred while they were playfully dunking each other at the lake. Bobby got some water in his lungs and almost passed out. A severe warning from her father followed and the matter was dropped. In her mind, however, the realization that she had almost killed her brother frightened her and left her no peace, while also depressing her because she felt so guilty. Her parents quickly detected a changed mood in Linda and two days after the incident called me long distance for advice.

The swiftness with which these parents took action made it possible to reduce these symptoms after four more telephone calls ranging over the following ten days. Twenty minutes was the average length of our conversations.

The parents were directed to proceed at once to challenge for Linda the thought that she was blameworthy for this accident. It was enough that the child had seen how careful she must be in the water henceforth. That in itself was a valuable lesson which might even save her life someday in the future. If she would think only of how it happened and how she must play in the water the next time, she was doing all she could to correct her mistake. Mother and father were further instructed to remind Linda that no one is perfect and we therefore expect people to do bad things. She was to make no excuses about the accident, but to like herself even though she had the close call. Had the baby brother died, this would have been even more necessary to make her understand lest she be burdened with a crushing guilt for the rest of her life.

"Tell Linda she's a wonderful girl and you and dad love her and that she must not blame herself ever." I instructed.

"Won't she perhaps make too light of the incident, Dr. Hauck, if we play it down?"

"I don't want you to play it down but I don't want you to make it too big either. Teach her better habits of playing in the water instead. Take the two children down to the lake and let them, for instance, experiment with holding their breath under water. Show them how far they can wade out before they're over their heads, and show them the various kinds of horseplay which are potentially dangerous. That wouldn't be underplaying it by any means and it will immediately cancel out any fears of the water they might be developing right now."

"I see, and you want me to be nice and loving at the same time?"

"Yes, never hold a moment's anger aginst her. Actually order her, if necessary, not to blame herself. You might say, 'Linda honey, I want you to stop hating yourself right now. Do you hear? It's too bad what happened but it turned out okay. Now enough of this calling yourself mean things and thinking about this all day and night. We're up here to enjoy a vacation and that's just what we're going to do. Do you understand me?' "

Children can be *ordered* to stop their self-blaming just as they can be ordered to brush their teeth.

It was necessary to remind the parents to praise Linda lavishly for all the other nice things she was doing daily. She minded well, helped around the cottage, and continued to get along famously with her brother. Rather than take these behaviors for granted, her parents were advised to pay much attention to them and thereby give actual proof to their belief that she was still a lovable person.

Depression, being as common as it is with us humans, should be far better understood than it is. Until now our understanding of this emotional state was not only limited, but confused. Nothing really clearcut has appeared in the literature which makes this problem easily explainable. Now, however, because we psychologists are beginning to focus on thinking and attitudes rather than on all the feelings we had since childhood, it is possible to show any person how he is today depressing himself with his neurotic thinking, and precisely what he will have to do to overcome this painful emotional state.

To begin with, I find that there are three causes for depression, not one. They are: self-blame, self-pity, and other-pity.

The depression always looks the same regardless of which method the person is using to depress himself. One can weep over one's terrible mistakes (self-blame), weep over not getting what one very much wanted (self-pity), or weep for all the miserable souls in the world (other-pity).

To help a child over his depression, or even to overcome your own for that matter, it is first necessary to understand which form of depression he is suffering from, and then to convince him that it is neurotic and irrational to behave in the manner which is bringing on the depression. That is to say, we must convince ourselves first, and then attempt to convince the child that we should never blame ourselves, that self-pity is pointless and unnecessary and can be overcome, and that feeling sorry for others is also wasteful and unnecessary. Let us first look at the arguments against blaming oneself.

Self-blame and self-hatred are sensible and justifiable only if it were literally possible for human beings never to make mistakes or to misbehave in any way. Then one could intelligently say, "I did badly and I really didn't have to. I could have avoided it since I am super-human and do not ever have to make a mistake. If I do make a mistake it must be because I allowed myself to err."

No one in his right mind will insist this makes sense for humans. We are less than super-human, and we cannot help doing badly sometimes. At the beginning of a learning period, in particular, we invariably do badly. At the outset our piano playing is atrocious, our French pronunciation is awful, the child's eating habits are sloppy, and their manners needs constant correcting. Despite the fact that this is so obvious it is literally amazing to see and hear so many people blame themselves for doing badly when they are in the early stages of learning a skill. What I am urging the reader to understand is the fact that we must, have to, will, cannot avoid, shall, and cannot help break things, kill people, steal, beat, gossip about, and lie to others. Because we are human we have no choice as humans but to do all the horrible things people have been doing for centuries. This doesn't mean that you or I will do the senseless killing or robbing, or lying. It does mean, however, that *someone* must do it. If you insist this is not so you are arguing for the existence of heaven on earth, a preposterous idea.

If we were to accept our weaknesses as people we would not say of ourselves or our children the next time we or they behaved badly, "We should not have done that." Instead we will say, "It would have been so much better if you had not done that. However, you did and that's regrettable. But because you are imperfect you must show that imperfection in your thoughts and actions. And when you scribbled on the wall Jimmy, you were showing us just how human you are. Your mother and I don't like dirty walls, however, so we'll have to figure out a way to keep you busy without ruining the house. Maybe we'll have you scrub off the dirty marks in the hope that you will learn not to do that again. Maybe you'll have to pay mother for cleaning your mess, and you can pay her out of your allowance. Or, if scribbling is something you really believe you have to do to be happy perhaps we should get a pad of paper and have you color each sheet completely until you think you've gotten it out of your system. Whichever method we use will be geared only to correcting your problem, not blaming you for having it. We love you but we dislike your problem and habit."

Can you as a parent or guardian do this regardless of what the misconduct is? Instead of accepting Irrational Idea No. 3: There are actually bad people in this world and they should be severely blamed and scolded for their wickedness, can you think of the misconduct as the result of stupidity, ignorance, or disturbance? If you can you will find yourself calming down considerably, those around you becoming less tense, and both of you in a more intelligent frame of mind to do something about the misconduct. In short, never blame anyone, or yourself, for anything, at any time, any place. When a child learns to think of himself as a born mistake maker, but one who *can* change and learn if he does not blame himself, he will be free of depression which is caused by self-blame.

The second cause of depression is self-pity. This is caused by believing Irrational Idea No. 4: The idea that it is awful or terrible if one does not get what one very much wants. Again, it is only natural to feel blue and down in the dumps when it rains on the day we planned a picnic, or when a girl cannot have a new dress for the prom while all her girl friends do have new dresses. It is even more natural to pity oneself when confined in the hospital for a summer or to fail in landing a job because the applicant just before you was just hired. Doing the natural thing doesn't mean that it must be the *inevitable* thing. If we will only teach our children not to blow up events out of proportion and to accept injustice and frustration as a fact of life they will be far more stoical about adversity and at least not make matters worse by depressing themselves. Despite the fact that it may not seem so at first glance, most unhappy events can be tolerated fairly well if we will only make our minds up to it by challenging the neurotic notion that it is *awful* not to get everything we want.

The following is an excerpt from the first and second counseling sessions with a teenage girl who came to me for relief of her depression. Although this client is somewhat older than the group to which this book generally applies, the principles employed in her recovery are the same as for younger children but the conversation must be geared to the age of the child.

Therapist: Yes, speak.
Client: I don't know what to say other than the fact that I am depressed.
T: Okay. What are you depressed about.
C: Well, number one, my combo broke up. Number two, about three weeks ago the guy I had been going with for years all of a sudden decided that was it.

T: Un-huh.
C: Mainly it's that, and I just don't quite know what to do. I have no sense of direction. Even though I have a good job I get these extreme ups and downs emotionally and most of the time it's been mostly down. I have lost ten pounds in three weeks and I have about three or four hours sleep a night. I can't sleep, so it's a hassle. I've tried everything. My close friends all tell me to think about each day at a time and take it easy and just be happy. It's just easier said than done for somebody else to say there are certain things I have to do. It's just trying to figure out how to do them. I just don't know. I have tried everything. I've tried going out and having a good time with my friends and last weekend I took off to the city and drove around to see another musical group. It was all fun for the time but as soon as I got off to myself and started thinking about things again, I started living in the past and got depressed again.
T: Thinking about what in particular?
C: Just the fact that all of a sudden after two years Joe has just gone. I mean that's all there is to it. And there are no ifs, ands, or buts. I have got to learn to accept it but I can't.

The client has stated the problem in a nutshell. What she does not see, however, is that she is depressed because she pities herself over the loss of her job and her boyfriend. It is now time to get her to see her dynamics as clearly as possible, and although this is only a short way into the first session, there is no reason why we should not proceed straightaway to the heart of the matter.

T: So what do you think is depressing you now?
C: What I just told you about, the combo and Joe and getting my head where it ought to be.
T: What do you think is preventing you from taking reversal in a sensible. mature, and undisturbed way. Why can't you do that?
C: I wish I knew why I can't. I don't know.

T: May I suggest something? I'll tell you about depression. I'll tell you the ways in which people get depressed and then you tell me what you are doing. All right? We'll see if we agree.

There are essentially three different ways that I know of in which people become depressed. The first is when they blame themselves a great deal over their mistakes. They have done something wrong. They have behaved badly. They have committed a sin and they think it is perfectly sensible to hate themselves for it, to run themselves into the ground over it, and never forgive themselves for having erred. That would be one very, very fine way of getting depressed.

The other way is when you feel sorry for yourself, when you pity yourself, or when you think you have been a living doll and you've done your level best. It's usually then that you feel most deserving of the fruits of your hard labors. But when this stinking world very unjustly does not give you what you think you deserve you think it's awful, it's too bad, and boo-hoo. See? That feeling sorry for yourself, the self-pity, is another very good way to get depressed.

Now the third way to get depressed is to pity somebody else. You see some kid with a broken leg and your heart goes out to him. Or you see some fellow who is blind and you are ready to cry for him. Or you see a dead dog on the highway and you are all shook up over that. When you feel excessively sorry and disturbed over others you can be just as depressed as when you pitied yourself. It all looks the same even though the reasons for the depression are somewhat different. Which of those methods are you using to depress yourself?

C: I don't feel sorry for anybody else. And I don't think I feel sorry for myself. I am not sure. I don't necessarily feel sorry for myself like saying, "Oh poor me." The whole world is down on me." That's not true. Life is fine and everything is beautiful basically. It is just that right now I guess it is just trying to adjust to the fact that, well, love is a habit in some ways and it is

just trying to adjust to the fact that all of a sudden I am on my own again completely.
T: All right, are you blaming yourself for that?
C: I don't think so.
T: All right, are you pitying him?
C: Not at all. Joe knows what he's doing.
T: All right, then what is left?
C: Just the fact that I feel sorry for myself.

Interestingly enough, she could not see this obvious fact. The rest of the first session was spent allowing her to ventilate and question this interpretation. Toward the end of the session an attempt to summarize my impressions was made and a homework assignment was given.
T: Okay, what have I been saying?
C: Quit feeling so sorry for myself and look up and say there is another day coming and face it.
T: Yes, and since he has stepped out of the picture and you can't have his attentions any more, what should you go out and be doing?
C: Just living life and letting things happen the way they are going to happen and quit worrying about what is going to happen and what isn't going to happen. Just cross every pathway that comes along.
T: Do you think you can do that?
C: I'll try. I think sometimes I have actually been able to fight it.
T: Yes, when you are not feeling sorry for yourself and crying in your beer over the fact that you've busted up.
C: It's just an up and down.
T: Only because you let it be.
C: It just seems like such a waste that it ended.
T: It is regrettable that it ended. It is not a waste. You enjoyed it at the time. It is like saying if you eat a meal and say, "Isn't that a waste now that it is gone!"

C: So I am supposed to look forward to another meal.
T: Of course. What's a meal for except to enjoy it? What is a relationship for except to enjoy it, and if it finally ends someday for one reason or another, through death, through moving away, through disinterest, all right, it won't kill you. It is over and you had something for a while and be glad you did. Keep your mind off that sad stuff. Instead of thinking how horrible this whole thing has been just tell yourself it's just one of those things and that you're not going to pity yourself over it. It is bad enough that you lost a boyfriend so why should you get depressed and make the whole thing worse? The worst part of your whole problem is not that you lost Joe, it is now what?
C: The fact that I am depressed.
T: Sure. Joe is not even responsible for the greatest share of your difficulties. It is you. Why? Because you pity yourself. If you can stop the depression you can easily put up with the separation. Okay?
C. Right.

The second session took place three weeks later. The client learned her lesson extremely well and was actively fighting her self-pitying. She was asked what caused her changed mood.
C: It was like a lead balloon being dropped on my head. A great awakening. That's what it was. It just happened. I don't know how. I was sitting back watching television and it struck me. I thought how much time was I going to spend wasting feeling worry for myself when I had so many things to do. And that was it. I just started being myself again and that was great.

She then related how she resumed several old relationships, joined another musical group, and had new dates. She slept well again, put on weight, and lifted her spirits to their former exuberant level. She summarized her insights in the following way:

C: The heck with all these problems. Everybody has problems. I've got problems right now but I am not sitting around and worrying myself to death over them. I am not ignoring them either. That would be just going to the opposite extreme.
T: That's right. You have to pay attention to your problems, and when you have done as much as you can about them, get your mind off them and start to live. Correct?
C: Sure. Sure you can't do anything more about a problem than to think it through and try to solve it. It doesn't have to bring you down and make you depressed just because there is a problem.
T: True, that's often done by feeling sorry for yourself and blaming yourself over the problems.
C: Right.

She was further questioned to make certain that she understood my reasoning and was not making a good show of it. It appeared indeed that in one session she was able to grasp the principles of R-E T and to apply them to herself. We wound up the session with the following exchange.

T: I congratulate you. I think you have done a very fine job.
C: I want to thank you for your help too. You have to have somebody give you some kind of an idea.
T: You did the work and followed the instructions very carefully. I think you worked on it very hard and gave it some thought, all of which was essential.
C: But I never by myself would have thought I was feeling sorry for myself. I was too clouded in my thinking to even think that at all.
T: That's why counseling is a very good thing occasionally, isn't it?
C: It is a good thing. It really it.

The third way we can become depressed is by other-pity, that is, to feel excessively sorry for someone else. And why not? If we can depress ourselves by pitying ourselves, why should it not create the same feeling if we pity others? This form of depression almost invariably results from believing Irrational Idea No. 10: One should become upset and disturbed over other people's problems and disturbances.

Before the reader decides that this is a heartless and unfeeling attitude to adopt, it is important that we do not confuse concern with over-concern. As long as we are concerned over the welfare of others we can often do great things to help relieve their troubles. But, the moment we become overly concerned, when we begin to ache inside and become depressed, then we often effectively remove ourselves as possible agents of relief for the people we want most to help. I once counseled a social worker who daily visited the ghetto neighborhoods and who identified so closely with the misery she saw each day that she became dejected, apathetic, and depressed. The following day after telling herself she *should* be upset over all the woes she had seen the day before, she was so unhappy and blue that she could not go to work the next day.

Here we see the foolishness of pitying others. Instead of rolling up one's sleeves and pitching in to rectify a wrong we moan and groan about how others must be suffering, and then become disturbed ourselves.

Children have a way of feeling indifferent to the distress of others or of feeling extremely sympathetic. When they do the latter they can become as depressed as if they had blamed or pitied themselves.

The removal of this depression can take the same form of debating with the youngster as if he or she were pitying himself or herself. The specific points to bring up in defense of not pitying others are naturally somewhat different from those employed against self-pity, but the parent or guardian who needs to fight this emotion can easily do so in many instances by rereading the excellent case of the girl who pitied herself and applying the same techniques to the problem of other-pity.

Other-pity is more an adult problem than it is a child's. For this reason an illustrative case will be omitted and the adult is advised instead to focus on the first two forms because of their greater frequency. If we can rid our children of just the first two forms of depression we can rest assured that they will be largely free of this emotional ball and chain for the rest of their lives or at least relatively so.

Special Reminders about Worry and Depression

1. It is usually necessary to fight two ideas when we see worry, for we must not overlook the false ideas which create the depression. The first is created by idea 1. we should worry over possible mishaps, and the second by idea number 2. one is worthless unless competent. Often the worrying cannot be relieved until the child feels he deserves the relief. While he severely blames himself he has no thought but to punish himself and this his worrying does only too well.

2. Simple assurances to the child that the feared tragedy will not happen are too weak in most cases to remove a big worry. This assertion is furthermore distrusted by the child since he doubts that the adult can really be so sure of the future. And he is right! The full possibility must be recognized that the worst *can* happen even though it might be unlikely, but that the youngster need not be wrought up in either event. If he does not master *that* knowledge he will always be subject to further attacks of anxiety whenever a danger threatens.

3. The charm of using reason in the control of disturbing emotions lies in its wide applicability. It can be carried out not only by the professional counselor such as the psychologist, psychiatrist or social worker, but by the minister, teacher, probation officer, doctor, etc., not to mention the parent himself. As was demonstrated, it could also work via telephone conversations. In addition, it is commonplace for reasoning to be taught through lectures, tape recordings and the written word. Such is its charm!

4. The sooner a disturbance is given attention the sooner and easier it is brought under control. Far too often parents neglect a problem until it is so irritating it cannot be ignored. The effort needed to correct this delayed situation is needlessly increased and is a great disservice to the child who must learn to slay dragons when he could have gotten by with swatting a fly.

5. Fighting a depression requires a non-blaming philosophy as we have already shown. If done correctly it is theoretically enough. A forceful catalyst, however, which every supervisor of children must never ignore is the need to reinforce this process with much praise, compliments, and flattery. Parents who feel uncomfortable at this because it is "phony" or "embarrassing" must grit their teeth and do their best. With practice it becomes easy.

6. Getting the child to focus away from the dreaded event can be facilitated if he is given homework assignments such as calling up his friend, reading a book, playing a game, going to a movie, etc., whenever possible each time the thought depresses him. The mind can focus on one subject at a time. If it is counting numbers it cannot also be thinking of illness. The moment it does, it could be forced into concentrating on a poem. The more time spent away from the worry the weaker its influence is, provided, of course, that the irrational idea itself is kept under question.

7. Any adult who uses rational therapy to help children will soon find his own disturbing emotions dwindle. He will become more and more convinced of his own irrationalities as he challenges those of the child. This by-product has the added benefit of making it easier for the child to live with the adult the more such counseling is done.

CHAPTER XI

Discipline

There are roughly four reasons why children misbehave: they want attention, power, revenge, or to be left alone by showing a disability.[1] Remember these four reasons because so much of what seems confusing with children can suddenly become clear as light when analyzed for one or more of the above motives. Furthermore, in trying to understand misbehavior it is a good idea to get into the habit of asking oneself. "What is the child trying to *achieve* with this behavior?" Do not ask immediately *what* is making him upset, but instead ask yourself what his *goals* might be. This is extremely important because the remedy to the problem is sometimes wonderfully easy when we see clearly what the purpose of the behavior is. For example, there may be numerous reasons why a child feels rejected and inferior. He may show the symptoms of these feelings every time company comes to the home by being an annoying little brat. It does the parent little good to ask what caused the behavior (at least while the company is present), but it does considerable good to ask what the child is hoping to accom-

1. Dreikurs, R., Children: The Challenge, New York: Meredith Press 1969.

plish by such behavior. In this case attention-getting would be an obvious possibility and its treatment would simply be to ignore the child by not rewarding him with a lecture since this too focuses all attention on him.

This point is perhaps made more clear when we view the behavior of a rebellious female adolescent. She is doing badly in school, is madly in love with an unsavory fellow, and has become unexpectedly hostile and disobedient toward her parents. This is a common enough syndrome these days. The parent, in attempting to comprehend such behavior will ask such questions as, "What is the matter with the child? What have I done wrong? What is bothering the girl? What problem is she disturbed by?" None of these questions are inappropriate, they are simply not as precise and on target as the following question would be: "What is she expecting to happen and to achieve by dating that boy, or by getting poor grades? She has a very precise purpose in mind. I wonder what it is. It must be one of the following four: attention-getting, power, revenge, or using sickness as a way out of responsibility."

In such instances it is usually power which is the motive behind such behavior. When the parent sees the behavior as an attempt by the child to show them that he or she is stronger than the parent and that the child is saying, "I'll do what I want and you can't stop me" then and only then does all the misbehavior have an explanation and then and only then is there an obvious solution. More of this later.

Before studying the symptoms and correction of each of these problems it behooves us first to think differently about punishment as a form of discipline. A swat on the seat of the pants is mild physical punishment and must surely be used by every parent throughout the world at some time during the rearing of his children. Severe beatings and hard spankings are another matter entirely and should unequivocally be eliminated if at all possible. Almost without exception nothing good happens when a child has the daylights beat out of him by an angry parent or guardian. The most intense kind of hatred toward authority is built up in this way, and the lowest forms of self-concept are also created in this manner. A child who is slapped hard on the face or who is strapped or put over the knee and given more than a few swats is going to hate others and *himself*. Why himself? He thinks there must be something awfully wrong with him to be treated so badly. If he were as good as others he surely wouldn't be treated with such contempt and hostility.

The whole message behind a severe beating is "You are bad. You are no good. You are so bad in fact that only the most severe measures will correct you. And besides, you deserve the worst just because you are so worthless."

Try now to imagine what the child feels like after such treatment. What does he think of himself? What confidence does he now have in his ability? How deserving do you think he feels about success and the good things in life? How cooperative, I mean *really* cooperative do you think he will want to be with you after such treatment? And lastly, how do you think he is going to get others to treat him? Will he seek out others who will treat him kindly and fairly? Or will he seek out those who will keep his image of himself alive, by teasing him, finding fault with him, and by dominating him?

The more we convince a child that he is no good the more he believes he is no good. This usually makes us all the more angry and we give him hell again. He is further convinced that he is even worse than he thought *and behaves like it,* and we become even more incensed. And around we go. We blame the child and convince him he's no good. He believes us and must then act in a no-good manner. And then we are surprised at what he is doing to us. We never seem to realize we are getting back what we dished out. The parent who tells his son, "You dumb-bell, you'll never amount to anything. You're going to wind up in the gutter," is not only scolding his son, he is *predicting* for the boy what he can expect in the future. More than likely his predictions will come true.

A better way to discipline must be used, one which omits all harsh forms of punishment, both physical and psychological. The penalty method has already been mentioned and is good to use when a swat on the seat is enough, but for complex problems the following method is advised. It is called logical consequences.[2]

There are two consequences to our behavior: natural and logical. A natural consequence is getting burned when touching a hot stove. A logical consequence is flunking a class after not studying. If we have reasonable stability we will almost invariably learn after suffering from either of these consequences. The natural consequences do not come from us, they come from the environment. Logical consequences, however, can often be contrived by us, and must be, in fact, in order to change some of the irritating behaviors we daily confront. The combination of logical consequences and rational-emotive therapy can provide the motivated parent with just about all the techniques he needs to do a fairly good job of rearing a child.

DISCIPLINING THE ATTENTION-GETTER

Doing absurd things for attention's sake stems from the feeling of being no good unless one is approved of by others. This neurotic philosophy should always be counteracted all through childhood. There are numerous instances, unfortunately, when a long sermon is not called for and will do no good whatever. At such times the best method is to ignore the behavior. An attention-getter is getting what he wants when we laugh at him *and also when we scold him.* This too is attention and he'll settle for it if it is the only kind he can get.

---

2. Dreikurs, R., and Grey, L., **Logical Consequences**, New York: Hawthorn, 1968.

When a child plays with his food and his parents interrupt the supper conversation a dozen times to tell him he must finish, that the food is good for him, that it's expensive and the starving children in Europe would love to have what he has on his plate, they are simply showering him with attention and making a prima donna out of him. He can sit back and bask in all the fuss which is being made of his eating habits.

Instead, it would be so much more sane to offer him a choice. "Joe, if you don't want to eat that's all right with me honey. I'll take your plate now and you can go out to play. However, you won't have anything until breakfast. You decide what you want to do."

This puts the responsibility of his behavior on him and any consequences he suffers thereafter will be his fault, not yours. After all, it's what *he* chose. Naturally you must watch that he does not snack before bedtime or he won't be experiencing the consequence of not eating at supper time. Do this calmly each time, give him his choice, and nature will take care of itself.

The child who is always showing off whenever you go visiting can be asked to choose between behaving himself or staying home. Do not scold, spank, of lecture. It usually will do no good and in fact can easily reward him with more of the attention he so desperately thinks he needs.

The saturation method can also be used to get the attention-getter to calm down. The child who has been yelling at the top of his lungs all morning can be told, "I suppose there must be some great need for you to yell as you do so go right ahead and yell as loudly as you can for five minutes. If that's not enough you can have another five minutes." If he gets tired of shouting before the five minutes are up, urge him on and if he has had enough, assure him that you're always willing to give him all the opportunity to yell if he wants it. The same technique can be used with gum chewers and match strikers. Give them all the gum they want, let them chew to their hearts content before doing anything else and give them the same reassurance that they can repeat this any time and give them the same reassurance that they can repeat this anytime the urge grabs them. Match strikers have been "cured" in this way after striking about three boxes of matches.

All of this should be done in a friendly way, not vengefully and spitefully. When it is done in the latter fashion the behavior will continue because the parent will have engaged in a power struggle with the child and that is nothing short of asking for trouble. Do not stand over the child while he is chewing his head off or he will feel he is being punished and then he will fight you by chewing more than is good for him and will possibly make himself sick.

Some of the more common problems and the logical consequences which I have found successful in reducing or eliminating them are listed below.

1. The poor eater. Give him normal portions of food but take the plate away when he is disinterested in eating. Nothing else for the remainder of the night.

2. The wiggler at the table, or the child who is up and down from his chair. Take the chair away.

3. Quarreling children at supper table. Ask them to take their plates and finish the meal in another room of the house.

4. The child who forgets to take his house key with him to school, or who forgets his lunch. Don't bring him the key or the lunch to school. Let him do without until he decides to remind himself.

5. Two quarreling siblings over a household task. Assuming they won't go so far as to kill each other, leave the room, or even the house while they work out their differences. Lock yourself in the bedroom if you have to. All they want is to suck you into their squabble and make you settle the dispute. This is often impossible to do fairly and anyway, will win you one friend and one enemy.

6. Not going to bed on time. Make them stay up as late as you do but force them out of bed for school in the morning.

7. Spending the allowance impulsively or long before another payday. Refuse to make any loans. Make them work on special tasks if they really want extra money.

8. Not doing the dishes. Don't cook for them until they finish the job. Cook only for you and your husband.

9. The late-comer to meals. Let him cook his own or settle for peanut butter sandwishes (which he can make himself).

10. Horsing around in the car while it is in motion. Pull over to the side of the road and don't proceed until everyone has settled down. Don't say a word.

Get the idea? Action, not talk, that's what makes such a wonderful impression. The child sees for himself, in an unmistakable manner that certain consequences will follow certain undesirable behaviors. The less screaming and lecturing, the better. Use your ingenuity and you can deal with most behaviors you want to correct. And you can do it at minimum cost to you. But *do* it. You're not doing your child a favor by being firm and then telling him he's a louse. On the contrary, you are only training him to dislike himself and to be undisciplined. Do him the favor of showing him firmly the results of his behavior and you will be doing him the greatest favor. The woman who invariably ran her son's forgotten lunch up to school was doing him an immense disservice. The kinder method would have been to let him go hungry several lunch periods so he would learn to be more responsible. Being responsible is far more important than having a few lunches.

HANDLING A POWER STRUGGLE

This is one of the modern phenomenon we are seeing more and more of. Children are increasingly insistent upon getting their own way and will go to ridiculous extremes to do so. A capable child who brings home poor grades may simply be trying to show his parents that they cannot make him study if he does not want to study. Or, if you should successfully threaten him so that he does resume his studies he will more than likely frustrate you in some other way, perhaps through drugs, staying out late, or shoplifting. When it looks like normal warnings aren't working and the usual penalties don't change the behavior either, it is absolutely necessary for the parent to pull out of the power struggle and *admit defeat*. Is this difficult to accept? Then listen to this. I have known persons who flunked out of school to spite their parents. Others have allowed themselves to go with bad gangs and be caught doing something illegal because they knew the parents would be sick about it. Some girls even get pregnant and have one or more illegitimate children because the mother or father would be thoroughly humiliated and hurt by such behavior. But the child does it nevertheless because he or she has to prove that they can do as they please.

"But," you ask, "why should we parents admit defeat?" For the simple reason that you cannot win against such determination. A child is after all still somewhat stupid compared to an adult and he makes winning so blamed important he doesn't care what the price is. You and I are usually not so reckless and will not ruin our lives just to prove a point. The child can and does do this all the time. Therefore, instead of locking horns with the knuckleheads it is much wiser to back away in the following manner and offer them a choice again.

"Look Mary, I give up. You have me. I thought I could make you clean up your room but now I see that I was wrong. If you don't want a clean room there's no way I can really make you have one. All the fighting we do over that room isn't worth it. So if it's so important to you to live in disorder, do so. However, because your father and I do care what others think, I can't allow you to bring your girl friends to that room unless it is cleaned up. And if you bring someone home to listen to your records upstairs and the room isn't made, I'll just ask her to leave." I want you to make a choice between having your friends up to your clean room or having a disorderly room. You choose."

This extricates the wise parent from the struggle and leaves the responsibility for what happens up to the child. She will of course test the parent to see if she really means what she says. When handled calmly and firmly, however, the girl will see in short order that mom means business. And if mom is nice about the whole thing and doesn't lose her control, miracles can happen.

If the problem is not a dirty room it might be picking up clothes, or hurrying to get dressed so the family doesn't have to wait before going out. Fallen clothes can be packed away (so can discarded and unpicked up toys). And if the child is old enough to be left home when he is not ready to leave on time, leave him without saying a word. The same is true for the child who is always having to be urged to get ready for school. Get out of the fight mother and father Say no more and let the girl go to class late. That's the logical consequence of fooling around while getting dressed in the morning or of not getting up when called. A few such experiences will soon enough teach the youngster what he can expect. If he doesn't like the consequences of the choices which *he* has made he'll have no one to blame but himself. That's the beauty of not fighting and sermonizing with them. It leaves them holding the bag. And this is what is meant by pulling oneself out of the power struggle.

DEALING WITH REVENGE

The more hostile we are toward our children for the spiteful things they do to us, the more justified they are going to feel about performing other spiteful acts. The best remedy for this behavior is to detach oneself as much as possible from being hurt by vengeful acts. Use the method of logical consequences, and at some time show them that you do not think they are bad for behaving badly. Always remember that children behave badly because they lack intelligence (are stupid or mentally retarded), lack knowledge (don't know how to perform an action correctly because they have not been shown how or have not had enough practice), or they lack maturity (are so upset at the time that they can't help acting in an upsetting way).

The worse a child is the more love one should give him. It is very difficult to continue being angry at someone who returns love for hostility. This hardly means that a guardian should calmly sit by and let a boy or girl make mince meat of them. I have not suggested being passive, merely nice. One can still be firm and loving at the same time.

I once counseled a mother who complained about being cursed at by her ten-year-old boy whenever she would not give him his way. At first she slapped him and scolded him soundly. This did not work. In fact his behavior turned for the worse. When she decided to leave the room and leave him to his swearing he finally felt it was futile, that she meant what she said when it was pointed out to him that, "You're angry with me, I know. However, I'm not making you angry, just frustrating you. If it makes you feel beter to curse me I don't suppose I can really stop you. But I don't have to listen to it." And away she would go. In short order the boy would talk himself out and come around in a more receptive mood.

The mother was, of course, delighted with this change and quickly recognized the secret to her success. She gave him no further cause to hate her and she did not play his game by getting involved in a useless lecture. The wise parent should often ask himself whether or not the behavior he is protesting against always calls for drastic measures and whether a more detached attitude wouldn't work just as well. In this connection it is important to remember Irrational Idea Number 10: One should be terribly upset and disturbed over other people's problems and disturbances, and Irrational Idea Number 12: The idea that it is vitally important to our existence what other people do, and that we should make great efforts to change them in the direction we would like them to be.

THE REMEDY FOR THE CHILD WHO USES DISABILITY AS AN EXCUSE

Playing sick before going to schol is an old trick with youngsters and can be expected in most families at some time. To accept this behavior at face value rewards the child for playing sick and encourages him to resort to some sort of disability whenever he is again confronted with a task. One of the best ways to deal with this problem is to take the child literally and treat him accordingly. If he claims he cannot go to school because he has a stomach-ache then he should be put to bed in a very sympathetic way and treated like a sick child. The curtains should be drawn to reduce distractions and thus permit him to sleep. Coloring books are also denied him, as are television and radio. When school is out he cannot have visitors because he is "sick." One day of this is usually enough for the malingerer.

Some children play weak or scared by not answering questions put to them. They hope to impress their parents with the difficulty of arriving at a decision and they hem and haw endlessly—finally bringing the parents to the point where they yell and shout at them to make up their minds and say something. This only plays into their hands because the exasperated parent is likely to make the decision for the children—precisely what they were hoping for.

Instead of falling for this trap it is again wiser to take the situation from another viewpoint and to assume that the child would not mind missing something. Does he or does he not want to attend his friend's party? No answer. Fine, he'll stay at home. Does he want another pork chop? No answer. He gets none.

In this way we teach the youngster to face his responsibilities and to make decisions. He is rightly afraid at times to forge ahead with an action that may turn out badly. However, to get him off the hook and permit his supposed disability to make him more dependent upon us only creates a more frightened child. Life is full of uncertainties and the sooner he learns to risk failure and to act despite this risk the sooner he will feel his own strength and trust in his own judgments.

SUMMARY

The facts about discipline can be listed briefly:

1. Keep yourself under control at all times if possible.

2. Do not care too much for the welfare of your child because you will push too hard and he will fight you and spite you for it.

3. People will usually (though not always, of course) make sound decisions if it is left up to them—perhaps after they have made several bad ones. This may be a big price to pay at times, but so be it. To become involved in a neurotic struggle with children so they won't make a big mistake is often as harmful as the mistake they would make if they had their own way. After all, adolescents do manage to give up drugs, they do return to college and get their degrees, and they do divorce when the marriage was obviously a mistake. Thank God!

A CASE STUDY ILLUSTRATING SEVERAL FORMS OF MISBEHAVIOR

The woman in the folowing conversation came to me about physical symptoms caused by emotions. This is our second session, and we take up the thread of our talk part of the way through where she begins to talk about her son.

C: I've been getting resentful with my son. He can put me in a position emotionally the same way his father could.
T: How?
C: Just by little things. It's irritating. Say that he wants something to eat but he doesn't know what. He won't say what he wants. I find it very annoying. Maybe it's something else, I don't know. When big things come up, this is simple. It's the little things. He broke his thumb in school the other day. He has to have a doctor's appointment the first of next week and I figure this could be his responsibility. So he says, "You call, you're my mama."
T: How old is he?
C: Seventeen. I know you'll tell me to stick to my guns and let him make the appointment. But if I don't make it, the appointment won't get made.
T: Okay, then don't make it. If he doesn't care about his thumb why should you?
C: He'd tell me I'm his mother and should protect him.
T: That's right. Let's have a big baby here. When does his responsibility start? Watch him now. He'll bother you, then you'll be weak and give in, wont' you?
C: I may not give in but there's going to be a bad emotional reaction.
T: Like what?
C: By withdrawing, probably. And by being being bitter.
T: And you? How will you feel if you let these maneuvers work on you? Won't you become bitter also and complain of being manipulated by his scenes? The thing you have to ask yourself is why do you have to be manipulated by your boy? So he has a scene. Let him have a fit if he wants to. It's not your problem. One of the best ways to help him grow up is to let him be frustrated a few times. Let that thumb hurt. Let it get infected. When it hurts enough and he sees that you aren't going to make that call you can be sure that he will be forced to

do so himself. Being firm about it will teach him what he can learn to expect.

C: Ever since he was a child he has always been able to twist me. He'd just cry "Mom" and I would just melt. Much of that is gone now but some has still hung on.

T: Sure, but you're still feeding it from time to time. You either feel guilty over it or you think it's easier to give in to the damn thing than it would be to fight him on this. See?

C: No, he makes me feel guilty.

T: Guilty? Like you're a rotten mother. But that's what you have to think through real carefully. Are you a rotten mother for being firm with a seventeen-year-old and expecting him to grow up? How does he make you feel guilty?

C: By accusing me of not being a proper mother.

T: Just accusing you is all it takes?

C: Yes, it sure is.

T: So how are you going to fight that the next time he comes out with "Man oh man, you're some fine mother." What are you going to say to yourself?

C: Just say that I'm not, that this is the best thing for him. I will be doing him more harm by not being firm than by being firm.

T: Why would you be?

C: Well, because he'll continue to be more dependent on me.

T: What's wrong with that?

C: He has to be independent of me as an individual so he can grow up to be his own person.

T: Why must he?

C: So he can be mature?

T: Why does he have to be mature? Why can't he be an immature baby for the rest of his life?

C: Because, down deep he would be unhappy if he doesn't become mature.

T: That's the point. What you've been doing is making him a

happy person *for the moment*. But in the long run he becomes a sniveling, complaining, snotty, spoiled brat. So you're really not helping him except for the moment. It gets him off your back and that's all. All you've got is a happy little youngster at this moment. You're not preparing him for later on. Oh no, here he is, seventeen years old and you're still falling for his strategies. You've got to watch out for that don't you? After all, after you're gone and he's on his own, what kind of a life is that boy going to have then?

C: This is what I keep telling myself to do, but my actions belie me.

T: I don't think you've thought it out carefully enough, that you're not really being a good mother when you give in to every one of his lousy complaints.

C: Yes.

T: A good mother will teach him some frustration tolerance. One of the most important lessons you can teach him is to let him do a thing by himself even if you can do it for him. Don't do it for him. Let him be frustrated, it's good. He's going to have frustrations for the rest of his cotton-picking life. See? Teach him frustration tolerance by frustrating him. Tell him it's going to be the story of his life and if he can't stand frustration his name is going to be "Mud." Why? Because he's going to be miserable. Makes sense?

C: Uh huh.

T: So what are you going to do the next time he comes along with his typically, childish, demanding behavior?

C: Tell him he's got to make up his own mind and bear the responsibility.

T: And if he comes back with those accusations of you being a lousy mother?

C: That's too bad. But it's his problem and if he wants to face the future he'd better start now since I won't be around forever.

T: He may get tougher with you when you take a firm stand. Did you know that? People pour on the steam when their old methods don't work. If he's been only a little bit fresh with you before, watch out because he may get really vicious. But if you're careful and refuse to do battle with him, and if you let him suffer the consequences of his neurotic behavior he may have a good chance. But be careful that you don't try to force your will on him. If you do you'll find that he will have you but good. You'll never win if you get into a power struggle. For example, nothing you can do will make him take care of that thumb of his unless he wants to take care of it. So stay out of it.

This mother unwittingly was playing her son's games. He was constantly playing the role of the weakling who needed to depend on mama, and he was fighting her with every weapon he knew of to make her continue doing so. Sometimes his behavior was motivated by attention-getting, sometimes to show her she had no power over him, and lastly to demonstrate that he had a disability and she should not expect him to grow.

She learned her lesson well because by the very next week she reported improvement in the relationship. The boy tried his old tricks but mama did what she said she would and calmly let him be. And because he could not get her to act in his behalf in all the minor ways he once succeeded at, he began to change. A phone call from her several months after we terminated reassured me that the progress continued nicely.

CHAPTER XII

Lack of Self-Discipline

One of the least spectacular problems facing a parent is teaching his child self-discipline. Spectacular problems are odd problems, such as phobias, sleep walking, delinquency. Self-discipline is seldom viewed as a problem in the same way ulcers nightmares, and temper tantrums are. Yet it is a problem and therefore, becomes the proper domain for the psychologist.

The undisciplined life is a wasted life. At the very least it is almost bound to be an unproductive life. Accomplishment can be gained only by hard work which overcomes boredom, impatience, and discouragement. Self-discipline is the one most important ingredient, next to ability, in the story of success. All the ability in the world is worthless unless it can be disciplined to function. Some people work well only when that discipline comes from without. But as soon as the external authority is removed they fall again into states of helpless unproductivity. The greatest rewards of life can come only to those who have mastered their indifference and laziness. They have disciplined themselves. And they are truly in charge of themselves.

Problems with self-discipline arise from two mistaken notions we are taught. 1) If we don't like something, or it is unfair, we shouldn't have to do it. 2) It is easier and better to take our pleasures immediately rather than deny oursevelves and get pleasure later.

Brad, a lad of fourteen, was doing so badly in his history class he was afraid of flunking. I had worked on another problem of his and this being cleared up he now raised this new one.

"I can't seem to get myself to do my history work. And I know if I don't do better I'll have to take the whole course over again next year. The whole subject is so boring it just kills me to study it. I keep wondering why I have to take it anyway."

"What thoughts do you have when thinking about doing history assignments?"

"Oh, I think how much I hate it, and what I could be doing instead of reading history. I keep wondering why I have to take it, what good it'll do when I'm a business major anyway."

"Brad, none of what you've said so far can account for your deep resentment toward this subject. So far everything you've said is true, or could be true. What we're looking for is the false belief or beliefs you hold. When we find them we'll know what's making you react so neurotically to just simple history homework which you're easily able to do."

"What did you mean about those reasons not explaining why I fight doing my homework? If I hate a subject and can see no value in it, doesn't that explain why I fight it?"

"No. For one thing just strongly disliking something is not going to make you avoid it necessarily. If your folks ask you to sing a song for company next week you may dislike doing it very much, but you'll do it if I know your father. And you may not think it has any value either. That's still not going to make any difference. Because your dad wants it, you'll do it and try your best at it. To understand our reasons for unpleasant emotions we must find out the nutty stuff we are telling ourselves, the false beliefs, irrational ideas, the nonsense we believe. Then when we can show ourselves we have *really* been believing nonsense, the disturbing emotion will evaporate."

"I just told you all I can think of. I wouldn't know what else I'm telling myself."

"I can think of something, the conclusion from all those thoughts, namely, that just because you don't like the task, can find no value in it, think it's unfair to be assigned work in it, therefore you *shouldn't have to do it!*"

"Well, isn't that true? Why should I have to do it?"

"Why the devil shouldn't you?"

"Because I don't get anything out of it and it won't help me in business."

"So who says you shouldn't have to take any courses you don't like or don't add to your knowledge of business?"

"No one I guess. But still why should I *have* to?"

"Because the school is making that a condition for your diploma. Now I agree they may be wrong about making it one of the conditions, but that's their mistake. Until you can correct it you're stuck with it. So to answer your question, you should have to take history because that's how you're going to get your diploma. If you don't want the diploma then of course, there's no reason why you should have to take history or any subject for that matter. And besides, why shouldn't you have to do something simply because you don't like it? Since when is this world so considerate of all our feelings that we have to be pleased at everything we do?"

"That would be sort of impossible wouldn't it. Apparently I am giving myself a hard time over history because I feel it is unjust to do something I dislike and see no value in? And if I see that this belief is wrong I won't get steamed up over this work?"

"Try it and see. And in the meantime don't keep telling yourself you hate it when what you realistically mean is you dislike it. No wonder you refuse to do the work after you keep telling yourself all day long how terrible it's going to be. It's hardly *that* bad, now is it?"

"I suppose I do make it sound like murder itself. And that's why I feel so awful too, isn't it."

"Who wouldn't feel positively awful after telling themselves all those loathesome things about history. Tonight when you tackle your next assignment tell yourself, 'Okay, here goes with history. I'm not going to like it but so what. If I don't make it out to be horrible, I'll feel better about it. And even if I see no value in it, if I want to graduate, this is part of what it's going to take. Maybe I won't get much use out of history, but the diploma will help me get a job at work I do like. And besides, who am I that I shouldn't have to do something just because I dislike it? Come on now, get to work, get it over with, and you won't have to take this fool stuff next year.' If you do this each time you develop your old resistance, you'll soon calm down and see some sense."

Three weeks later Brad was indeed applying himself to this distasteful task. He learned gradually to challenge his nonsensical thinking until the homework became less and less odious. It was not entirely surprising to me when he remarked a few weeks after that, that he was now finding history to be a much more interesting subject than he had even believed it could be. He got past having to remember names and dates and his keen mind delighted in the analysis of human events, and how they have shaped his present world.

In summary, the correction of this problem in self-discipline lay in getting this boy to see that there was no logical reason why everything he was asked to study had to be interesting and that whether it was or not, it eventually would lead him to a more desirable goal (graduation) and if that's what he wanted he would simply have to pay the price.

This may seem so common sense-like to the reader as to be unnecessary or unworthy of comment. Yet, millions of people fail to see this very good sense unless it is pointed out to them and they learn to *remind themselves* of it when they become resistant and start sabotaging their sensible goals.

More important than the previous reason for poor self-discipline is procrastination caused by the belief that an immediate reward or a moment's pleasure is better than delaying the reward for a later pleasure. To delay unpleasant work simply because it is unpleasant lets it mount up to a later time when there is perhaps twice as much to do. The belief that "letting it go for now" is easier on the person is entirely fallacious. It is harder even though for the moment there may be a brief but temporary feeling of relief. The housewife who thinks she is taking the easy way out by not doing her dishes today has two loads tomorrow. The young man who does the "easy" thing by not calling up a girl and risking rejection also experiences brief relief but spends a lonely evening at home.

Many parents make this mistake over what is really "easy" with regard to rearing and training their children.

Mr. Tufts complained bitterly about his son's laziness. Elmer was expected to help run the tractor at planting time, milk the cows on those mornings his father was otherwise occupied, and do other odd chores on the farm. His performance was generally poor and his dissatisfied father found himself with much more work on his hands than he had counted on.

"I get so disgusted with that boy I feel like smacking him. You'd think he'd learn after a while, but no; I have to do everything myself."

"You mean he rebels against the work?"

"No, he's willing enough, at least he was a few years ago. But now he drags around like he's half dead. No life in the boy. And so I wind up doing the job myself. It's easier that way."

When Mr. Tufts said the word "easier" I was able to diagnose the problem immediately.

"What do you mean by "easier,'" I asked?

"I mean its easier to do it myself than to spend all day trying to show him how to do it. I've got work to do."

"Sounds to me like it wasn't the easiest thing to do after all. I wonder if you didn't in fact, do the hardest thing by doing it by yourself and not taking time out to instruct him."

"But that would have taken forever."

"Hardly forever, Mr. Tufts. Granted it might have taken an uncomfortably long time, it would still have been 'easier' to take that time each time since eventually Elmer *would* have learned and could be of great assistance now. Instead, you did the hard and harmful thing by making it easier on yourself *only for the moment.* Now you still have the job ahead of you that you could have handled then—training your boy."

"Hmm. I didn't think of it like that before. I can see what you're getting at. I made it easy on myself at that time without realizing that Elmer was still going to have to be taught sometime. And if I didn't do it then, why I'd have to teach the boy someday anyway."

"Now you're thinking. So what would you suggest to correct this problem?"

"Let's see now. If I give him something to do and he has trouble with it, show him over and over again how to do it right rather than take him off it. After all, he can't learn the job if I do it for him can he?"

"Hardly."

"And if I do that he'll catch on sooner or later and will eventually be a help to me. Yes, by golly, that *would* be easier in the long run. Why didn't I think of that? It's so simple I'm embarrassed." he said with a smile.

"As I said before, you didn't think of it because you unthinkingly believed it was easier to do the job yourself at first (which was true) but you didn't think about how hard you were making it on yourself in the long run."

Mr. Tufts reported back at a later date he had begun to take all the time needed to train Elmer and although it slowed him down noticeably at first, he was already beginning to have things easier after one month since Elmer was now effectively helping out. In addition, the many little successes the boy was experiencing were helping him gain confidence in himself so that he was coming alive and acting in an enthusiastic and energetic manner.

Whether it be reducing, breaking the smoking habit, learning an instrument, or even applying these sound psychological principles all of them require hard work, and constant practice. To avoid them may be ever so pleasing for the time being but this relief is short-lived and only delays the truly worthwhile rewards we are striving for. It is not easy to discipline ourselves, but it is easier than not disciplining ourselves.

CHAPTER XIII

Undesirable Habits

We are creatures of habit, and how fortunate for us! Without them each task would require the same concentration and effort each time as it did while it was being learned. But once learned we tie our shoes while whistling a song, play piano without looking at the keys, and drive a car while conversing with a passenger. Habit permits us this freedom.

This freedom is ours, however, only as long as we are calm. When, for an instant, the habit fails to work, and we worry over the accidental failure, or slip of habit, the mechanism which allowed the habit to run automatically will go awry. Some people tend to become further alarmed at this point and make too much of this temporary malfunction. Then, the tension so generated does even greater damage to the once wonderfully automatic and smooth performance. The delicate balance is now thoroughly disturbed and a once smooth habit looks like a fine watch that has been pounded with a hammer.

Whether it be the writing of one's name, speaking, or controlling the bladder, and no matter how long they have been performed smoothly, they can all falter from time to time and if this accidental error is regarded as a catastrophe, the habit will suffer and truly begin to seem catastrophic. Let us look at several undesirable habits and see how they started and what steps were necessary to bring about the smooth, automatic performance which was suddenly lost.

Bedwetting

Sally was referred to me by her mother who related in an open and honest fashion how thoroughly disgusted she was with her fifteen-year-old adolescent for having wet the bed continuously for the past ten years, "practically every night." I tried to find out when it first happened and if Mrs. Platt (Sally's mother) could recall what happened on that occasion. She answered that she could remember nothing in detail, only that ever since having the problem she has mildly resented the extra laundry, and was now experiencing increasing embarrassment for her daughter's childish habit.

"Why, I shudder to think what the relatives are beginning to think. They must wonder what's wrong with me for raising a girl that still wets," she said with great shame.

Noting this and other emotional reactions like it, I felt the mother was almost in as much need of counseling as her daughter (who was not present) and at once proceeded to reason with her.

"Mrs. Platt, I can certainly sympathize with your problem and the extra work it means for you, but aren't you upsetting yourself needlessly?"

"Needlessly? I should say not. Am I supposed to ignore it and pretend it's just wonderful that Sally can never accept an invitation to a slumber party, or that it really doesn't matter that she can barely spend a night away from home unless we bring our own sheets and rubber mats and what have you? Why if this continues she may not even want to get married to say nothing of not going away to college. Yes, doctor, I think I have good cause to worry and be upset."

I then asked, "Do you mean that you will be helping her problem by becoming upset?"

"No, no. I mean I can't help but be disturbed over her problem. I know it won't help her when I worry, too!"

"Well, then we agree on one thing at least."

"What's that?" she asked.

"That your worrying doesn't help."

"And what don't you agree with?"

"That you have to be disturbed just because she has this unfortunate problem," I answered calmly.

"You keep suggesting that I could remain calm about Sally's difficulty and that all I have to do is decide it by will power. This I certainly can't agree with, but even if I did, that still has nothing to do with Sally and that's why I'm here, to help her," she replied with noticeable indignation.

"Again, Mrs. Platt, I can only agree with part of what you just said. I hope I can show you two things: first, that you, not Sally, is upsetting you, and second, that it would help Sally a great deal if you'd learn how to handle this problem calmly. More than you realize you are helping this bedwetting stay alive by worrying so much about it."

This had a quieting effect on Mrs. Platt, who thought for a moment and then asked sincerely, "You seem to know what you're talking about but I confess I still don't follow you." Then with a deep sigh, "What did you mean by your first statement that I, not Sally, was upsetting myself?"

"Just that, Mrs. Platt. The only pain Sally or anyone can cause you is physical pain. Now Sally has not hit you, or tripped you, or assaulted you in any way. She's wet her bed. This can cause you more work certainly, but I hardly think that's what's bothering you since if you had another child you'd have that much to do and you probably wouldn't mind it."

"That's right. I'm sure the extra washing, although I dislike it, is not what I'm worried about. It's what the wetting will mean in her life. That's what I'm afraid of."

"And what are you telling yourself about that?" I coaxed her on.

"That she'll never be happy this way. That the poor girl doesn't deserve that kind of a life and she's going to miss out on a lot. That it's a crying shame she can't enjoy her adolescence like other girls." Mrs. Platt went on with a long list of regrets, grievances, and doomsday predictions until I interrupted her.

"Small wonder you're upset," I concluded.

"I should say so. Even thinking about it now upsets me."

"I don't think you understood me," I cautioned.

"Sure I did. You were saying that now you could understand why I was so upset when we see what Sally will suffer."

"Not quite, Mrs. Platt. You still seem to believe the unfortunate life Sally has ahead of her is the reason for your disturbance."

"Yes, and you said, 'Small wonder you're upset.' "

"But I didn't mean it as you took it. Sally's predicament had nothing to do with your getting upset just a moment ago."

"What did then?"

"It was what you *said* a moment ago. This and not Sally's troubles disturbed you." I could see she was puzzled and so proceeded to amplify this thought. "Your feelings are determined by your thoughts. If you are saying all sorts of angry things to yourself you will soon feel angry all over your body. If you think jealous thoughts you will feel jealous. And if you think alarming and unhappy thoughts, how will you feel down here in your body?"

"Alarmed and unhappy, I suppose," she answered a bit mechanically.

"Right. And that's how we create our emotions all the time, whether positive and happy, or negative and moody. Our thinking leads to our feelings. Change our thinking and we change our feelings. You're upset presently about Sally's problem. Think differently about it and you'll feel better in short order."

"But how will that help Sally's problem even if I manage to calm myself down?"

"It may not help at all. At least, however, you won't be disturbed by it."

"But that wouldn't be right would it, not worry about her problem. I'm afraid I'd feel guilt over being a poor, unconcerned mother if I didn't take her troubles to heart."

"I haven't said you should be unconcerned or indifferent. By all means take an interest in her troubles and work very hard to help her over them. But, until she overcomes them, why make yourself sick with worry and anger?"

"In other words, I could be concerned about Sally without being nervous and unhappy about her, too?"

"Of course you could. And if you would, Sally might learn to be less alarmed by her problem. If she were, she'd relax more and *then* she might stop wetting."

"So my overconcern and anger may be making her more nervous which in turn only makes the wetting worse. I can see that, but frankly, Dr. Hauck, I still don't understand how I'm supposed to stay so calm when I know in my heart I feel awfully sorry for her."

"It isn't because you feel sorry for her that you are upset as I also feel sorry for her and I'm quite calm about it. Instead it's because you falsely believe that you have no choice in the matter merely because you have a problem. Lots of people automatically make themselves disturbed almost each and every time they have a problem or face a crisis. They erroneously believe the problem causes them to be disturbed. What they don't see is that they alarm or anger themselves *after* they get a problem."

"You're separating the problem from the emotion which usually follows it. Can you do that?" she asked.

"Of course we can. Don't tell me you get upset over every problem you have!"

"No, certainly not," was her thoughtful reply.

"Well how is it then that you remain calm and undisturbed over some problems but not so over others?"

"Some problems are bigger than others."

"Wrong, that's not why. If you'll think back over your life I'm sure you'll find numerous examples where you were faced with a big issue and you handled it smoothly and without disturbance."

"There were times when the children were sick that I marveled at my composure, that's true."

"Well then, if all problems must lead to emotional disturbances, why weren't you upset then?"

"I don't know, why wasn't I?"

"Because you weren't having alarming or upsetting thoughts."

"Perhaps not, doctor, but if I didn't the situation probably wasn't as alarming as Sally's is at the moment."

"No matter how alarming a situation is, it is still our choice whether or not we will get disturbed by it. Nothing can cause us pain unless it's physical. You have been upset in the past because of what you told yourself after something happened. Look at it this way: suppose we call Sally's bedwetting problem A. Now this is not injuring you physically in any way. But when you see that she has wet and you think over all the difficulty she'll have in her life, then you say things like, 'What a pity; poor girl; oh, how horrible; what a mess to clean up; such a bad girl; how embarrassing; etc.' Then you say one final thing: 'Because these are true and this is a hopeless, horrible problem, I can't help but get disturbed, embarrassed and angry.' Let's call these silent sentences inside your head B. If you get yourself after a time to believe these thoughts as being true then you must become upset, and let's call that C."

Mrs. Platt now smiled triumphantly and declared, "But they *are* true!"

"The first part of those sentences may be true although I wouldn't even agree totally to that. But the conclusion, 'Therefore, I must be upset' is totally false. But you wrongly believe that problems and frustrations can *cause* emotional disturbances, and believing *that,* it only follows that you must become upset. Until you see how false that is you'll always upset yourself *over* your problems. Notice I did not say your *problems* will always upset you."

"Then you're saying nothing, whether it be my husband divorcing me, or my children getting into trouble with law, can make me upset?"

"Remarkable isn't it."

"Surely you don't mean it literally. People are bound to become upset over some things like death."

"Granted, I would expect most people to get upset many times in their lives. However, this still happens because they are disturbing themselves with their false thinking, not because the things happened in the first place."

"That's awfully hard to swallow although it seems to make some sense. Suppose I go along with you for the sake of argument, what could I do not to get upset?"

"Seriously question all the false beliefs you have at point B. Once you convince yourself these beliefs are false, untrue, and nonsensical, you'll relax. Suppose you go into her room tomorrow morning and see her changing her sheets. Tell yourself this time, 'Poor child, she wet again. What a pity. Well, there's little I can do about her problem apparently except remain calm. She's not perfect and may have this the rest of her life, so what good will my getting upset accomplish? Thank goodness she's not crippled, or a serious delinquent. Things could be much worse, so let's look at the bright side of it. Life must go on.' "

"Now," I continued, "if you had such thoughts, which I defy you to prove are not true, you could hardly be upset for long, now could you?"

"I imagine not. And even though her problem may remain unchanged, I can still act calmly and not create another one, is that it?"

"Exactly."

Mrs. Platt tried hard in the following weeks to follow this new instruction and often failed. However, in each following session I had with her we studied each failure, analyzed what she told herself just before becoming upset, taught her to think clearly about it and asked her to try it again in the coming week. In six weeks she was considerably more calm and accepting of Sally's problem and had some of the following comments to make on her last visit:

"Sally has been coming along so much better than before. Her wetting has all but stopped and I'm sure your talks with her have accomplished it. But I must say that my little contribution at home should not be ignored," she humorously suggested.

"By no means should we overlook it," I agreed ."You've done wonders with your own emotions and so Sally had only her own problem to think about instead of her's *and* her mother's."

"Oh, I wouldn't say I've done that well. But I am doing better. Once I could really see how I was talking myself into an emotional stew over poor Sally's problem I decided I'd just have to stop hurting myself with all those alarming thoughts at B and see what I could do about C instead."

"And what did you do about C?" I asked.

"Remained calm. That was the best thing I could do for it. And it was the only thing I could do. After all it was Sally's problem, not mine and if she were going to stop it, it would depend upon her, not me. Then I further convinced myself that no matter how severe a problem any of my children had, they could really not upset me unless I let them do so, and what good would that do?"

"So you stopped telling yourself that Sally had to stop wetting and that if she didn't, your worrying and wrath wouldn't change it anyway, so why not relax?"

"That's right, doctor. As you said, 'What you can change, change. What you can't change, accept philosophically.' And if I keep on thinking that way, I'll be a lot better off and maybe

Sally will, too. But even if she doesn't, my family dosn't need two emotionally disturbed people. One is enough." And she and I had a good laugh.

During those six weeks that I was counseling with Mrs. Platt I was also seeing Sally individually, weekly. She was not unattractive but deported herself in posture and conversation in such a defeated fashion that her fine looks and intelligence were completely overshadowed. I asked this fifteen-year-old girl to tell me what her problem was. Much of it was almost word for word what I had already heard from her mother. She then went on to explain how she had fought in vain over the years to conquer her symptom.

"I can remember the first time mother took me to a doctor to see what the matter was. He gave me some medicine and it helped from time to time but soon I was wetting each night again. We tried other doctors and tried all sorts of advice. Nothing worked. It doesn't matter whether I drink a lot or a little before bedtime. During the night I wet. Then I thought that if I could stay awake past the hour I usually had to urinate I'd have it made. So I'd stay awake as long as I could and then fall asleep exhausted. Then I'd wake up in the morning and found this hadn't worked. So I'd try to stay up longer, perhaps I hadn't found just the hour when I usually had to go. I used an alarm clock to wake me just in case I fell asleep. But it didn't help. In the morning I'd feel terrible and disgusted and would feel like beating my head against the wall." Here Sally sobbed.

"Maybe you're trying too hard?" I said.

"Too hard? How can anyone try too hard to overcome such a disgusting habit?"

"Sally, if you try too hard you'll make yourself nervous over possibly wetting. And once you're nervous you're more likely to wet."

"But, doctor, if trying very much doesn't work, trying less will work less also won't it?"

"Not necessarily, Sally. In fact, in your case I'd say don't try at all."

"What did you say?"

"I said, 'Don't try to stop it at all.' "

"But if I don't do something about it, I'll have it forever!"

"On the contrary. You've been working very hard to fight it in many ways except one; doing nothing. That's doing something, isn't it?"

"How can that possibly help? I must fight this thing or I'll never get over it. I keep thinking I haven't done enough," she pleaded.

"I must disagree. The more you insist on perfection the more of a necessity you make it. Then you'll become more tense and your body will become tense in strange ways and not operate normally. On the other hand, the less difference you allow this to be to you, the sooner you can relax and maybe the symptom will cease."

"This is confusing me, Dr. Hauck. How can I ignore something so terrible?"

"By convincing yourself that it's not terrible, and especially that *you* aren't terrible for having the habit."

"I am terrible. I hate myself for being this way."

"Then you'll never stop being that way," I protested.

"Why is that?"

"For the same reason I gave you before. You have wished so hard to be rid of this thing that it's no longer a wish. You've changed it into a neurotic necessity. And that's your big mistake; believing you have to control this habit."

"I do have to control it if I want to enjoy myself as other girls do, or get married. The way it looks now I may not be able to go to college. Don't you see why I have to stop it?"

"Yes, if you have to enjoy yourself like other girls, or get married or go to college. But who says you *have* to do any of those?"

"Oh of course I don't *have* to do those things, but then life won't be much fun without them."

"Perhaps not. Who says life must be fun?"

"It doesn't have to be fun, but if it could be, is it wrong to try to make it so?"

"Not at all, and if you thought this sensibly about your problem all the time you'd probably see it vanish. However, you're really not saying that at all. You think you are wishing for something, but deep down you are insisting on it, demanding it, making it a life and death issue. You have changed everyone of those natural, healthy wishes into sick, neurotic, perfectionistic demands. You've made the wish to enjoy yourself like other girls a need to enjoy yourself like other girls. Prove it. Who says you *must* enjoy yourself or have a good time? You do! You've convinced yourself that whatever you want you must have. Your *wanting* to sleep normally is perfectly fine and healthy. Your demanding that you must sleep normally is nonsense. After all it's not going to kill you if you wet for the rest of your life. You may not get married. That would really be too bad. But lots of women never marry and in connection with that, lots of girls never go to college. None of these wishes are truly necessities as you imagine they are. Suppose you had a physical defect in your bladder that made it impossible to control your urine normally. What would you say then?"

"I'd understand that, and make he most of it if the doctors couldn't do anything about it."

"And what would you say about not living like other adolescent girls, or marriage and college?"

"I'd just have to rule them out and accept that as a fact of life even though I didn't like it."

"Good for you. I'm sure you would. Well then, if wetting can't disturb you if it is physically based, how can it disturb you when it is emotionally based. You get just as soaking wet either way, don't you?"

"You mean," she said with insight, "if I can react to something in two different ways, then whether I am upset or calm does not depend on the thing but on how I see it or on how my attitude toward it is?"

"That's right. Your attitude now is 'I'm awful for wetting my bed since there is nothing wrong with me physically.' Then you feel awful because you think of yourself as a disgusting, dirty person.

"If it were physical you'd say, 'I wet my bed, but after all something is wrong with my bladder so what can I expect?' Then you'd be undisturbed emotionally. In the former case you'd dislike and blame yourself, in the latter case you'd accept yourself. In the former you would believe you *had* to stop wetting merely because it's possible not to wet, while in the latter you'd say, 'I can't help wetting and I'll probably never stop, so why worry.' Whether you would be upset or not depends totally on which of these attitudes you adopt, not on whether you stop wetting."

"And if I think like this I'll never be upset about anything?"

"Not about wetting obviously, but about something else that wasn't just perfect, yes."

"So I must learn first not to blame myself for having a problem and that will make me feel better emotionally. And if I feel better emotionally, I won't care whether I wet or not?"

"Partly correct. You'll always care, but not to the point of it being a necessity. That's what you have to watch out for: how much you make of your wishes."

Our hour was up. She said she'd think over what we said and report back in a week. The following interview showed no progress since she still stoutly maintained she absolutely couldn't accept herself unless she conquered the habit and she furthermore, couldn't believe that she could ever convince herself that it was not her problem but her thinking about it which was making her unhappy.

To these objections I merely hammered home with different logical arguments the same points stressed in our first hour. The third and fourth interviews were quite similar to the first two. On the fifth visit she came in with a big smile and opened the hour with, "After my last visit here, I went home and began to see that my worrying was really as much of a problem as my wetting and as long as I worried about it, I'd continue to wet. Well that night I was determined to ignore the whole thing. I decided not to wonder or care whether I wet or not. If I did, too bad; if I didn't, fine. Either way, I'd still have to set the breakfast table in the morning, go to school, play in band, come home, do dishes, homework and go to bed. None of these things would change a bit. Sure, maybe I couldn't sleep over to a girl's house, but if I lived out of town and didn't have a car I wouldn't be able to do it either. Or if we had a blizzard, or I broke my leg, or it was cancelled for some reason I also wouldn't be able to go and I'm sure I'd accept those misfortunes. Well, I calmed down and even remember thinking, 'Go ahead Sally, sleep and wet the bed all you like. It's a pain in the neck perhaps, but hardly a catastrophe as Dr. Hauck is always reminding me.' And it worked. I was amazed the next morning when I felt dry. Then suddenly all the things you've been trying to tell me these weeks made sense. And I tried it the next night and again it worked. In fact, it worked for six straight nights." She beamed with pride.

"You seem to have caught on Sally. Congratulations. Tell me, however, what happened on the seventh night?"

"I was just going to ask you about that because I wet last night again."

"Okay, let's do what we always do when we want to understand our mental problems."

"I know," she hastened to add like a school girl, "ask yourself what you've been telling yourself."

"And what were you thinking before going to sleep last night?"

"Hmmm, let's see if I can remember. I, yes, now I recall. I was thinking of how proud I was for not slipping six nights in a row and how proud you'd be of me, too. Then it occurred to me that if I could only stay dry just one more night, I'd make a perfect record of being dry one whole week—the first one I can ever remember."

"Ah hah," I laughed. "There we have it."

"How's that, doctor?"

"That's what caused you to slip; you made an issue of bed-wetting again. You let it make a difference. Notice, for six nights you went to bed with the idea that it didn't make a difference; you just weren't going to worry about it. So you relaxed completely and your body took care of the rest. Then on the last night you believed it was important *not* to wet so you worried whether you'd be able to make the record or not, and then you got tense. Now your body couldn't take care of itself, so you wet. Do you begin to see Sally how easily your thinking can cause this symptom?"

"Apparently so, but I find it hard to realize that I could actually bring on the wetting by such a small demand, you know, just to stay dry one more night."

"Perhaps it is a small demand, but it is still a demand, still overly important, still life or death. Any time you build your wishes into demands and necessities you're bound to have disappointments and troubles."

"I suppose I should never try to strive for perfection then?" she asked.

"On the contrary, strive for perfection all the time. Work always to do your best. But don't believe or convince yourself you *must* always succeed or that you're a worthless heel because you fail. When you fail, don't blame yourself. Just study your failure to see how you can avoid it next time."

"You don't want me to feel bad then that I couldn't be so perfect as to bring you this record of a whole dry week. Instead, you want me to think over carefully what I did to cause me to slip last night so that I can perhaps do better tonight. And that's what we've just been doing, isn't it?"

"That's right, Sally. Let's review it once more so you get

your assignment quite clear. The harder you try the more important a thing is to you. When it becomes a necessity you're likely to lose control over it. It doesn't matter whether we're talking about wetting the bed, playing piano or delivering a speech. If you believe you must be perfect and mustn't slip or be above all criticism, you're in trouble. The harder you try the worse your performance will be. So go home and reconvince yourself you don't *need* to be rid of this habit. Tell yourself you're stuck with it for the rest of your life and there is not a thing you can do about it. That will prevent your worrying. Then *if* it disappears you've got a bonus. However, whether it lets up or not is not the issue. You must learn to lump it because you just may not be able to do a thing about it."

Sally learned to think clearly about her problem and in the following weeks had her ups and downs. Some weeks she made little improvement, other weeks great improvement. In a matter of another month, however, she had stopped wetting almost completely. Then we terminated, fully expecting her to apply what she had learned. When I got a note from her several months later that she had just had her first slumber party the night before, I knew she had done her homework well.

Soiling

Personal cleanliness is one of the hallmarks of civilization. It is next to godliness. By further deduction we must conclude that uncleanliness is devilish, and the dirty child is a step away from evil itself; especially a child that soils in its pants.

Yet life starts out with a slap on the rump and the purchase of a diaper pail. All this, however, is well tolerated until the child has been toilet trained. Woe unto him, however, if he should, even for one instant, backslide to this messy stage once he has supposedly outgrown it. Then the tolerant mother and father become most intolerant and insist upon a perfect bowel performance. Yet this is unreasonable. Once a child has been toilet trained, he is still subject to an occasional soiling since most habits are learned gradually, not all at once. And when it appears that the habit has been well mastered, it is possible to slip back to the original behavior with an ease that is surprising. This reappearance of an old habit is called spontaneous recovery, and the misinformed parent assumes incorrectly that the child is not trying hard enough any longer, or that all former gains are lost totally and the work of recovery must start from scratch. None of this is true. When a child has learned his toilet habits well he usually stops thinking about them and relaxes. If he becomes unduly scared, or overly absorbed in play activity, or just fails to heed nature's call, he may soil. This is the spontaneous recovery; almost on its own the old habit has made a reappearance. This is predictable behavior and should not come as a surprise to his elders. It is better ignored for in all likelihood the child will not repeat it. If he is upset over it, the parent should assure him that old habits do not die totally and will sometimes visit us when we least expect them. The child should be shown that he is not blamed for this slip and he should be especially cautioned not to blame or dislike himself. With such an undisturbed, understanding and accepting attitude this minor incident can avoid becoming a crisis.

If the child makes no effort to control his habit and begins to soil regularly, most parents falsely believe they should then yell at him to make him realize what a pest he is, and will regret not having taken more severe measures in the first place. Again, they would be inefficient to follow such a course. They would be wiser to tell the child calmly that they want him to watch his habit more closely, that they do not blame *him* because he is soiling again, but they do not like his behavior and mean to see it stopped. If it does not stop, it will be penalized by slow degrees until the child would rather work on the habit to control it and have the penalties lifted than to have his occasional pleasure of playing and not going to the bathroom but suffering inevitable penalties later for this brief pleasure. These penalties, however, can only work if applied with love, lack of resentment, absence of grudges, and a sincere desire to *teach* the child a lesson rather than to gain revenge.

Mrs. Podds conferred with me regarding her seven-year-old daughter, Sharon. This child was soiling her pants persistently, sometimes as much as two or three times a day. No matter how often the mother cautioned her daughter, or actually forced her on the toilet stool, Sharon could just as likely as not mess her pants a short time later.

The child had been perfectly trained by the time she was two and a half and had not had an accident once from that time to the first week in school at the age of seven.

"Apparently," said Mrs. Podd, "Sharon was quite frightened by the newness of school, the routine, the surroundings, and all the new faces, and she got just plain upset and couldn't recognize when she had to go. Or she may have wanted to go but was afraid of asking her teacher. I really don't know how it started because she starts to cry every time I bring it up, and then, too, I'm beginning to think she never really understood how it happened, either. She was awfully upset at the time so I don't suppose I can expect her to know how she felt. And now, after seven months, she probably couldn't remember even if she did know at that time."

"You're probably right, but all this is not awfully important now. What we have to understand is how to get her to stop the soiling."

"That's what I want too, only I thought you had to understand the history of an illness before you could correct it. Don't the psychoanalysts always ask you about your childhood?" she asked with a smile.

"They do indeed, Mrs. Podd," I agreed, "but lately, research is throwing real doubt on how necessary it is to understand how something began in order to change it. You'll see as we move along on Sharon's problem that the first consideration I am interested in is whether her soiling is brought on because she has a physical problem, or an emotional problem, or both. After we know that, we'll know how to proceed and if it's emotional, you'll see how little attention I pay to her history. But let's take first things first: have you had her to a doctor for a check-up?"

"Oh, yes. That's the first thing I did. In fact, Dr. Langley referred me to you. He said you had helped some of his other patients. He couldn't find anything physically wrong with Sharon, so he thought it must be her nerves and wanted me to see you."

"For the time being then we'll have to assume this is purely an emotional problem. So let's start with what you have been doing until now to help Sharon stop this soiling."

"Oh, I've done about everything. Really. After I got over the first shock of that incident at school, I cautioned her about being careful the next day and even tried to get her to have a bowel movement before she left for school. She didn't have to go so I didn't push it. But wouldn't you know it, in the middle of the morning I got a phone call from the school asking me to bring Sharon a change of underpants and socks. And it's been something like that for months. Some days she's fine, other days she messes up to three times. And it doesn't matter whether I remain patient and understanding or treat her rough and punish her. I'm about at my wit's end."

Several statements she had made caught my ear. She spoke of being "shocked" when Sharon had her first accident; she clearly worried whether the same thing wouldn't happen the following day and took the precaution of trying to get her daughter to have a bowel movement before leaving for school, and lastly, she has not had a clear-cut plan as to how to handle her. First she was sympathetic, then angry, and finally confused. I had the strong impression throughout my session with her that she had never taken the accident as an accident but had let it become too important to her. Her very efforts to stop the soiling were now making that habit stronger, not weaker, and I now wanted to show Mrs. Podd how she was doing that.

I proceeded to explain the ABC's of emotion to her and how she, not Sharon, was creating the worry and embarrassment. "Of course," I continued, "you'll have to think about this a lot and practice what I've told you. Eventually you'll learn not to excite yourself even if she never stops this habit. I want you first to stop blaming her for messing so much."

"Oh, I don't blame her. I know she can't help it," Mrs. Podd insisted.

"I doubt that, or why would you be angry when she has an accident?"

"I'm angry at the mess and trouble she makes."

"Perhaps so, although I still question that. But let's assume that's true. Tell me, how does your seven-year-old daughter know that you're only angry at her soiling, but not angry with her?"

"Because she knows I love her. I've never given her reason to question my love for her."

"You said you got angry, disgusted, shocked, irritated. How do you suppose Sharon interpreted these reactions of yours?"

"You're suggesting that even though I may not have blamed *her* for the soiling, and been disgusted only with her habit, she's too young to know that?"

"That's what I was wondering. If you did something in the company of your husband and friends, and he were angry, shocked, and disgusted by what you did, what would you think his feelings about you would be?"

"That he was disgusted with me."

"Certainly. Of course, he might only be disgusted at what you did and not dislike you a bit for having done that thing, but you must confess it would be hard for you to know for sure whether or not it was only your action or *you* he was mad at. And if this would be so hard for you as an adult, you can well imagine how hard it would be for your inexperienced little girl."

"I think I see what you mean. That's why you insist, isn't it, that I must first learn not to upset myself over this problem since Sharon takes my emotional reactions personally, and thinks I'm mad at her and don't love her anymore, when I really do?"

"You put it very well. The calmer you stay over this whole thing, the better it will be for her. Then Sharon need only concern herself with one problem, her soiling. If you act like you're rejecting her, Sharon will have to worry about that problem also. Let's face it, one is bad enough."

She agreed and asked, "This still doesn't explain to me why she's soiling now and why this silly business got out of hand in the first place."

"Good. Let's discuss that. The very first time she messed her pants may well have been because she felt so uncomfortable in the new surroundings. Perhaps she had to go to the toilet but was too shy to ask for permission. Maybe she was so taken with all the sights and friends that she became overly absorbed in the events around her that she either didn't notice she had to go or hated like the dickens to leave her friends, or games or whatever it was she was engrossed in. As I said, it isn't very important why it happened just that once. What is more important was your shocked reaction the next time you met her."

"Why was that such a big thing? I've done it before, I'm sure, for other things she's done and we didn't get all these results."

"You're right, Mrs. Podd. It, by itself, might have passed by harmlessly. But it, plus your reaction the next day, and each time after, started to harden this simple incident into a neurotic habit. Had you been calm and not grossly concerned that first day, Sharon would probably have thought very little over the whole thing and remained calm. Then her body could have handled its natural functions in its own normal way."

"Yes. People become very nervous when something means too much," said Mrs. Podd with sudden insight. "And because she demanded that she *must* not soil again, she became tense, her body got short-circuited, so to speak, and it hasn't worked properly ever since."

"Now you're beginning to see this thing accurately. From what you've just said, what do you think the solution to her problem is?"

"I'm embarrassed to say it because it sounds so logical and yet I wonder if it could possibly be that simple."

"Let's hear it," I coaxed.

"Help her forget this whole business completely and get her mind off it."

"Bravo, Mrs. Podd. You've hit the nail on the head. Encourage her always to try to control her bowels, but always assure her it makes no difference how you feel about her even if she never learns that."

"If I don't show a reasonable amount of concern won't she perhaps decide that soiling isn't so bad?"

"I seriously doubt that she enjoys it. All along her problem has been caring too much; it hasn't been caring not enough as you've feared. Remember, she was putting all her eggs in one basket. Either she had to stop messing and become mother's sweet darling again or she had a slip and became a dirty, disgusting girl. Some choice, isn't it?"

"Yes, poor thing. I'm beginning to see why she was so fearful that she might have another accident. You suggest then that I ignore this business and always show her I don't blame her for it, is that it?"

"Half of it. You must also teach her not to blame herself. Even if you stopped criticizing her, she could still criticize and dislike herself when she messed. Then you'd be right back where you started. Say something like this the next time she has a bowel movement in her pants: 'Gee, honey, that's too bad. Come, let me help you clean up. It's not serious, and I don't want you to worry. You're still a fine little girl and I love you. This messing has nothing to do with that. And don't you blame yourself for one minute either honey. Sure, this is a dirty business and I'm sure you don't want it anymore than I do. Just because you have dirty pants doesn't mean you're a dirty, bad girl. Understand?' "

Mrs. Podd laughed, "Gracious, am I supposed to talk like that? My daughter wouldn't recognize me."

"Never mind that. She'll take a while before she really believes you, perhaps, but if you keep it up she'll probably think differently about herself and then relax. When she does that, the soiling may stop."

I saw Mrs. Podd two weeks later. She related that she had had a hard time realizing that Sharon was trying too hard not to mess rather than not hard enough as she had supposed. However, the more she thought about it, the more sense it made and the less anger she consequently experienced. She endeavored to pass this thinking on to her girl who responded very slowly at first. Still the mother held on and never once blamed her daughter again, and tried to get Sharon not to let it bother her excessively, either.

"It took about a week of the kind of treatment you told me of before I began to notice her let up somewhat. Now after two whole weeks I am pleased to see it diminishing even more."

"Keep up the good work, Mrs. Podd. There's no reason to suppose that she won't get more control as time goes by," I answered.

She then asked me if this habit would end abruptly, or whether she couldn't expect gradual improvement with occasional slips again. I explained to her how Sharon might very well make rapid or gradual progress, but would quite likely have slips from time to time because of spontaneous recovery of dead habits. I further pointed out that she must be very careful how she handled Sharon at that time.

"If you make a sudden fuss, and appear shocked because she suddenly starts to soil again you'll have to expect the same strong reaction from her you got when she soiled that day in school."

"In other words," she summed up, "I could repeat my original error and start this whole thing all over if I show the same surprise and disgust I originally did?"

"Right. Remember always that she'll be only too eager to be disgusted with herself. She really won't need your additional criticism. Assure her that she doesn't have to stop messing to become mother's darling. In fact, she doesn't have to do anything for that. It must be taken completely for granted."

"Yes, I suppose I have been putting conditions on my love. Don't soil and I love you; soil and I find you disgusting. That's not much of a choice is it?"

She came back in two more weeks to report that the soiling had stopped completely for several days, "almost a week, in fact" after our last session, over which she was delighted. However, Sharon started to soil again after that and for two days her mother kept my words in mind that this was a critical period in the correction of Sharon's habit. If she passed this test by keeping calm and unblaming, Sharon would probably recover. If she lashed out and showed her dislike for the girl, the battle would have to be won all over again.

Mrs. Podd managed herself well and this crisis passed. I made sure that she now realized that she would have to face the same crisis several times more perhaps. If she handled herself then as well as she did this time, all would go well.

Most adults do not appreciate the slow demise of a habit. They must anticipate its coming to life from time to time. It is true that old habits sometimes seem to end quite abruptly, but many have several spontaneous recoveries. These seem to come further and further apart in time as well as diminished in intensity. A month after our last visit Mrs. Podd reported that Sharon had stopped completely with her problem, but she was prepared should Sharon suddenly backslide one fine day.

Apparently she was prepared, for I learned some months later that Sharon had a few more accidents but they were handled with kindness and so each time her recovery became stronger until some time later it appeared that we had seen the last of her soiling.

CHAPTER XIV

Special Instructions for Parents

In my experience as psychological counselor over the years I have found that many adults show similar weak spots in their handling of children. Though they may read book after book on child psychology, or even follow the instructions of their counselor, the expected results do not materialize at times because one or more of the following points may not be clearly understood and are, therefore, sabotaging the sound work which is otherwise going on.

1. Do not change your tactics merely because the child seems at first not to respond differently.

Many times I have advised parents to do certain things with their children only to have them declare quite flatly that my suggestion would not work since they had already tried it. For a child who refuses to get to bed on time, for example, I might have advised penalizing him by not allowing the boy to ride his bike the following day. The parents might then report they had already tried this to no avail, and that he, in fact, had seemed totally indifferent to this penalty even when he was denied his bicycle for a week. The parents, seeing that their child seemed totally indifferent to this penalty, would seriously question if it was a wise move in the first place. Then, believing it would never work, they would retract that penalty and try another for a while. Again, if the child took the second penalty with an air of nonchalance the parents would go through the same doubt and eventually withdraw that plan in favor of a third idea, and so on.

What these parents fail to realize are three things: 1) the child may be acting and pretending indifference, hoping his parents will retract their penalty if he can show them it is not truly a penalty in the first place. He may say, "I don't care," and give every indication he has not been touched or frustrated in the least while secretly hoping and knowing he will win out if he holds out longer than his folks. Such "games" can be carried on for days. 2) To conclude that the penalty is not taking its effect merely because the desired behavior does not come about in a few days is false. This is often a waiting game, and those parents who are having this problem might well not give up so soon but rather continue a penalty for weeks if necessary. Holding out longer than the child may bring results which do not come in a few days. If the child has no special need for his bike this week we can hardly expect him to feel very deprived. However, if the penalty is maintained and later Junior is invited on an overnight bicycle trip with his friends, then we can see the obvious effect it might have. Only then will he realize he is frustrated. 3) If this too does not bring out the desired change in his behavior, rather than drop the first penalty and substitute a second, it would be wiser to keep the first and *add* a second. Now (to get back to our example) we will forbid Junior to ride his bike and to lose half of his allowance (or wash dishes alone each night, or wash the car each day, etc.). Then the parents should not be misled again if their son jumps at the chance to do this work and whistles all the while he works. This is a contest and he is using the strategy of "You can't make me obey by giving me a rough time. Look I love it!" Again, wait to see how he holds up after washing the car six days in a row. If nothing happens, keep the first two penalties in force and *add* a third and so on. If the parent will do this consistently and calmly (more on calmness later) they will almost always bring their child to the point of obedience. Of course, if all else fails the parent is best advised to resort to physical punishment as a last resort. Those childern who could not be moved through normal penalties will almost always succumb to physical force. It must be repeated, however, that this solution should practically always come after other solutions have failed, and it should be delivered without anger or blame.

2. Learn to penalize misbehavior which is a reaction to a penalty.

It seems that many adults are baffled when a child misbehaves while he is being corrected for a previous misbehavior. More than one set of parents I have counseled with have thrown up their hands in despair at not knowing what to do next when their penalties bring out even worse behavior. A few typical examples would be: the daughter who is forbidden to go out this night and told to go to her room as punishment, flings her coat across the room, speaks sharply and disrespectfully to her parents, and practically breaks the door to her bedroom when slamming it shut. Another example: a child is eating cake in the living room, dropping crumbs on the newly vacuumed carpet. To correct this behavior his mother takes the cake out of his hands, swats him once on the seat of the pants and warns him to eat at the kitchen table henceforth. To this the child reacts with a temper tantrum in which he throws himself on the floor, kicking his feet, making heel marks on the newly painted wall.

Parents who are at a loss when this happens reason that their discipline did not work in the first instance. Should they become firm again and possibly repeat what appeared to be a mistake? Too often they waver and show this indecision to their children who are good at spotting this weakness.

What is clearly called for is a continuance of the same firmness shown toward the initial misbehavior. The young lady who discarded her coat by flinging it across the room rather than hanging it up carefully has broken three rules of the home by 1) insisting on going out on a week night, 2) not hanging up her garments, and 3) slamming doors. To bring control back to this girl the parents would be advised to show her calmly which rules of the house she has broken and warn her what the penalties will be next time (if this has been the first such offense) or to enact the penalties for all three infractions. Thus, she might be grounded for one week for trying to sneak out without permission, she might be made to do the ironing for treating her coat so badly, and she could be asked to open and close her door fifty times very quietly.

Should this bring out further misbehavior the same principle should be followed. Thus, if she screams and curses and slams her door again, this new misbehavior must be dealt with as well. This will sometimes mean a very uncomfortable scene in the house, one which present-day parents often try too hard to avoid. However, this is a contest of wills and a display of childish, neurotic behavior and can and should be controlled if mother and father want mature, emotionally controlled adults some day. The sooner the child learns that he cannot act more impertinently when disciplined, or compound his poor behavior, the sooner peace will come to that family. Practically all families will have such contests and woe to those parents who are afraid to win them.

3. Histrionics look a great deal worse than they are.

It seems that one of the surest ways for children to reach the heart strings of their parents is to sob bitterly, pull their hair, throw themselves across their beds, and insist they are not being treated at all as humanely as all their friends are. Though this may sound humorous, when seeing a child go through these histrionics, the conscientious parent of today gets an actual fear that their child is becoming seriously emotionally disturbed and that unless they ease up on their rules the child will be so damaged in his personality that his adult life will be affected forever for the worse. This is not meant to suggest that these children are shamming these reactions. In the vast majority of cases they feel as bad as they sound and look. What the parent does not seem always to realize is that such behavior is not especially damaging. It is certainly hard on the child while she sobs her heart out over a frustration, but it will do little or no lasting harm. In fact, being too sympathetic and lenient merely because the child is reacting with histrionics can make these theatrics pay off all the more. Instead of this habit being weakened it will be strengthened because of its reward value.

A child's emotional scenes should never go ignored, however. It is reacting to a frustration in a painfully emotional way which to them is always justified and reasonable. As guardian, we must never overlook the possibility that we perhaps have been unreasonable in our expectations and rules. If so, modifying them in the light of our reconsiderations will be an act of justice. If our deliberation convinces us of the soundness of these decisions then calmly continue with the frustration but instruct the child along rational grounds that it is he, not the frustration, which is causing him the emotional pain. Many children will unfortunately not always learn to calm themselves even against the best reasoning in the world. They must be allowed their histrionics. The adult who is taking it all calmly can change this behavior much faster than the one who also becomes alarmed or angry. Histrionics are childish expressions from not getting one's way in the same way that temper tantrums are childish ways of showing displeasure or anger. The histrionics say, "Look how your rules have hurt me" while tantrums say, "Look at how angry I am because you made that unfair rule." If the frustration is a normal one (Sally can't go on a date tonight; Billy will have to do dishes today, etc.) the parent can well reason that none of these unpleasntries is truly serious and that their child had better learn to accept what they can't change regardless of how unfair the children may think it is.

4. Misbehavior will often worsen before it improves.

Children who are asked to change their behavior usually fight against this request. It is more comfortable to be the way one is than to learn new behavior even though one's present behavior is not particularly rewarding. It is natural, therefore, to anticipate a good deal of resistance from the child before he learns the new ways. His natural response to this pressure will be to intensify the old behavior. He will reason that what has worked in the past should still work today. If not, it's probably because he is not trying hard enough. If Bobby has managed to get his mother to let him go swimming every day because he has whined and pestered her, he will not whine less tomorrow because she has warned him that he'll be penalized for this behavior. On the contrary, having seen it work so faithfully in the past he repeats, with greater emphasis the method he has found so successful in the past. This is really a logical move on his part and should hardly baffle the parent. All of this simply means that before the child will change in the desired direction he will first increase in the undesired direction. This trend may in fact, reach explosive proportions, the child trying his past approach ever more intensively while the parents are continuing to penalize him with stiffer and stiffer punishments. There is nothing to be feared by this, it is a natural progression of events which will end by the child finally getting the message that unless he does change he will suffer more frustration when insisting on his own way than he would by giving in to his parents.

Some children take a good deal of convincing. They will simply refuse for some time to believe that mother will not back down if he (the child) keeps up his attack. It is during this period of discovery when the child is realizing for the first time his old tactics are not working that most parents lose faith in their handling of the child. They erroneously believe that this increased misbehavior must indicate they are doing something wrong. On the contrary, increased misconduct is often the first signal that we are on the right track. It tells us the child has been shook from his secure perch and is aware that new things are coming. It is the beginning of a contest, one which most parents can and ought to win most of the time.

5. Our disturbances are their rewards.

Unless an adult resorts to near brutality he cannot properly discipline his children when reacting to frustrations with emotional disturbances. Showing the child that he has succeeded royally in getting his parents all shook up is often so gratfying to the angry child that he will suffer any deprivation or punishment as long as he knows mother or father are not getting off scott free. This is truly idiotic of children or adults, for that matter, to make the suffering of the other person so important that one's own suffering is totally ignored. Sensible or not, it is a common, irrational human characteristic. Knowing this, the intelligent guide tries hard to remember 1) the ABC's of emotion (his children cannot disturb him); 2) that to become upset over the child would reward his misconduct.

An impersonal reaction to his misconduct leaves the child with no reward for his suffering. If mother calmly sends her daughter to bed for complaining for the umpteenth time about the food, the daughter may eventually learn to keep her complaints to herself unless she wants to go hungry (which is highly unlikely). If mother disturbs herself over this complaining, it becomes a weapon the child can resort to at any time.

Children can create such neurotic resentment against authority, for example, that a boy who must be at home by ten o'clock not to violate his probation will gladly waltz in late every night, completely oblivious to the fact that he risks hard penalties. Why does he do it? Revenge is sweet, so he thinks, and having seen his mother or father lose their composure a hundred times over his coming home late, having seen them worry and fret as his curfew hour drew near, having keenly observed their genuine suffering under those specific conditions, conditions which he can bring out whenever he likes; he senses a power to influence others which is new to him, and he foolishly feels that getting even is more important than correction, and that it is perfectly sensible to inflict a great deal of suffering on oneself because someone else has truly caused him a frustration.

Our children can frustrate us but never upset us. Let us react calmly to their undesirable ways and never let them see they have gotten under our skins. If we do not do this we become further at fault since we know these foolish children of ours will hurt themselves even *more* if they suspect we are losing patience, or becoming disgusted, or getting angry, etc. Being children they cannot help practicing these self-defeating maneuvers. As adults we *can* help the way we behave so the responsibility for maintaining our emotional control falls to us, not our children. The benefits are twofold: 1) we avoid the unpleasant experience of being resentful, anxious, or jealous, or whatever, in ourselves, while 2) we tend to reduce self-sabotaging behavior in our children.

6. Only a few of the child's many frustrations should concern the adult.

As parents it is our obligation to prevent children from experiencing prolonged or severe frustrations which could cause damage to them in their present or later life. We feed and clothe them so they can survive physically. We let them join clubs, have an allowance, go on school field trips and the like so they can learn to live socially with others. Most parents rightly feel that frustrating a child's social needs would be unhealthy.

Which frustrations are important and which can be ignored? Surely the parent does not need to concern himself over every wish the child has. Many mothers and fathers seem to have hazy notions of those frustrations they should act upon and those they can bypass.

There is no hard and fast rule anyone can set up which will serve as a ruler by which to measure the seriousness of frustrations. Each parent, however, is asked—no, urged—to question constantly whether they are placing their emphasis on the frustrations which need it. The child who complains about not having a dollar allowance each week instead of fifty cents can safely be ignored. The child who complains about always being blamed for everything that goes wrong at home deserves your closest attention. The girl who will not go to the next formal dance because she has already worn her dress twice might well be spanked and have her dress sold. The girl who complains that her clothes are so poor that she can never go to a school function at all should be better dressed somehow. Perhaps a dress from church donations could permit her to go. However, if she insists it must be a new one because she always gets hand-me-downs, she has become unreasonable and can nicely be told to sit home and stew about it.

From time to time in my practice I have come across women who feel they must be supermothers. They falsely believe that as a parent they must take it upon themselves to remove each and every problem the child might have. They have somehow lost perspective of what is and is not important. Being literally concerned over *every* frustration expressed by the child, these sincere mothers soon become so harried and dragged out, the glory and zest in motherhood is soon lost to the wish to drown or desert her children. If the child complains about not having the latest faddish sweater, this overly good mother who cannot stand to see her children suffer even slightly, buys her this sweater. She will buy her the latest sneakers, or buy him the currently popular bicycle, or baseball cap, even though these children already have similar items. Some mothers feel like failures unless they can prepare meals which are agreeable to each member of the family. Should there be disagreement over which of two salads, or potatoes, or vegetables should be served, the problem is solved by satisfying everyone, even if it means mashed potatoes for one child, fried potatoes for another, and a baked potato for a third. These women see nothing but evil in a frustration, and each and every one therefore, must be treated like a big thing, a catastrophe.

To gain the perspective to see more clearly how serious certain problems and deprivations are one must think of the problem in an historical sense. It cannot, for example, be a serious thing if a boy is not permitted to drive his dad's car for a week if one will only stop to think that 1) most children of the world today cannot have dad's car to drive, 2) until there were cars, this was totally impossible and was never done by any child at any time in history, 3) what's so awful about riding his bike (the world's most common form of transportation), or walking, or not going anyplace at all for that matter!

Women who lament how poor they are and how their homes lack most modern conveniences can surely take heart in the knowledge that their ancestors lived in caves, that most dwellings over the earth today are probably worse than theirs, and that if they compared their present shack with most neighborhoods of a few hundred years ago, their homes would be the envy of the village. Knowing that others throughout past ages have welcomed some of the situations which we consider frustrating can be very good toward giving us the perspective in knowing the important from the trivial. Those frustrations which endanger health, education, or ambitions can be serious. Those which interfere with our preferences, good times, and other incidentals can be ignored.

7. Practically all parents have regrets over being parents.

You simply cannot do a proper job of being a parent if you feel guilt toward your children. The guilt will make you: 1) fearful of being firm with them when they need it most, 2) oversolicitous and yielding as a cover up for your resentments, and 3) furiously unfair when these methods do not work. A child needs a guilt-ridden parent like he needs a hole in the head. It is high time that we adults faced up to our true feelings about our children. Only then, by being ruthlessly honest with ourselves, can we accept their frustrations and handle them constructively.

I do not know why we still nourish the ridiculous notion that children are a blessing all of the time, that their screaming must not be protested and that their inconvenience to our lives is insignificant. Let's face it, our children, wonderful as they are, filling our lives with purpose and pride, do so at a price. They require work, hard work to raise. They are expensive and we must deprive ourselves in countless ways to meet their needs. Quiet vacations, meticulous living rooms, sleeping late, all these and many more are often impossible when raising a family. To some these may not be frustrations at all. To others they are constant sacrifices. If so, own up to them and accept the truth you may be telling yourself silently, "I wish sometimes I did not have a family." More parents than are willing to admit this have these feelings from time to time. If they would accept these feelings merely as a fact of life which they can do little about for the time being, rather than feel guilty, their management of their children would run far more smoothly. You are not a wicked parent because you think your kids are a pain in the neck, you are merely being human and imperfect. Don't dislike yourself for it, merely do your best to reduce or minimize these frustrations. This will permit you to do several sensible things you would not do otherwise; insist on a Saturday night out without the children, hiring a baby sitter during a weekday so you can have coffee with your friends without your pesty, screaming, darling daughters to care for, etc. These are brief, but necessary vacations from the children which help you more easily to put up with tomorrow's certain headaches.

8. Go ahead, experiment. Parental mistakes are seldom fatal. Each parent steps into that role as a novice. Even with special training he or she will still require years before confidence comes through experience. Problems arise constantly which the parent must deal with for the first time. Perhaps Mrs. Smith's mother would know what to do about little Billy's stealing, but this is the first time Mrs. Smith herself has come onto the problem in her own children. Shall she spank him, hide the money, lecture him, or all three. Dare she shame him? Or make him feel guilty? Or would raking up the yard prove more efficient? She does not know for sure, and being uncertain but eager to do what is right she hesitates to do anything with conviction lest her mistake cripple the child emotionally for life.

Too much has been made of the enduring effects of behavior in childhood. Granted Mrs. Smith may well make a series of blunders (which can usually be avoided if she will read books, or seek professional help) but she need *not* fear these mistakes will be earth-shaking. Most blunders have small influence on children's personality unless they are repeated a number of times. Blaming a child for his behavior one time is like getting scratched on the knee once. Getting scratched on the knee several times a day, practically every day, is another story. Fortunately, the observant parent can usually have ample time to determine if his methods are improving things or making them worse. When he sees that he is getting nowhere he can practically always change his poor methods for better ones before any lasting harm is done his child. So relax, mother and father. Do not be afraid to use your ideas to manage your children. However, be aware of the great probability that you may have to shift gears and try other methods.

A worried mother once asked me if it was all right to be firm with her two sons when she was at someone else's house. She feared they might become very embarrassed and lose the free and easy feeling they had around strangers. She herself was a shy individual and so was delighted to see her sons did not have her problem. She was advised to go ahead and try it since one couldn't know unless it had been observed. Her suspicions were right in this case so she was simply told to warn them sternly before a visit how they must behave, and to penalize them after they arrived home. No harm was done by carrying out this unsuccessful scheme since the mother was quick to alter her ways when her good sense told her it was not working.

9. At any one moment your child could be praised far more than criticized.

One of the best ways to raise emotionally stable children is to love *them* despite their faults. Blame, which is here defined as a disapproval of the *person* and the person's *behavior* is the most important single factor in creating emotionally disturbed children. An excellent technique whereby a parent can avoid this dangerous habit of blaming is to remember that at the moment he wants to get angry and blame his child over a fault, he could, if he but stopped for a moment to think about it, find countless positive, good things for which he could also praise the child.

So Sonny walks into the house with mud on his shoes. Not only is this something one must expect from children, not only will getting disturbed not stop this problem effectively in the future, but this useless anger can be avoided by rightfully realizing that this one act of Sonny's in only one of a whole series of acts, and that practically all the others were worth your approval. For example, Sonny brought in all the toys you sent him out for. Why not praise him for that? He wasted little time in so doing. Shouldn't this be granted some recognition? He could have gone outside to fetch his toys, dropped half of them on the way back, dawdled all the while, and then stepped in the mud. In addition, he might have wanted to make mud pies but did not, or he could have sat on the furniture as well as walk over the rug, but did not. In short, we overlook all the things that did *not* happen but could have happened just as easily. Instead, we pick out the one imperfect part of his behavior and make a fuss over it thereby leading him to believe he does *nothing* correct or to our satisfaction. This is perfectly ridiculous and a moment's reflection can show this to any intelligent parent.

This technique can be very helpful in helping us avoid anger with our children. It does not of course, solve the problems such as bringing dirt into the house. This is a separate issue, but if the parent does not become resentful and blaming he can calmly teach Sonny what he has done and how he can avoid mud next time.

Another helpful hint which does wonders in controlling anger is to learn to address our children in terms of endearment. The mother who, out of habit, has learned to address them as, "Honey," "Dear," "Sweetheart," cannot flare up into a tirade too easily, unless she has forgotten all the principles of rational thinking.

Overcoming Common Problems

MAIL ORDER FORM

ARTHRITIS *Dr William Fox* Is your suffering really necessary	**£1.50**	☐
BIRTH OVER THIRTY *Sheila Kitzinger*	**£2.50**	☐
ENJOYING MOTHERHOOD *Dr Brice Pitt* How to have a happy pregnancy	**£1.95**	☐
THE EPILEPSY HANDBOOK *Shelagh McGovern*	**£3.95**	☐
FEARS AND PHOBIAS *Dr Tony Whitehead*	**£1.95**	☐
FEELING HEALTHY *Dr F. E. Kenyon* How to stop worrying about your health	**£1.95**	☐
GUILT *Dr Vernon Coleman*	**£1.95**	☐
HOW TO COPE WITH STRESS *Dr Peter Tyrer*	**£1.95**	☐
HOW TO COPE WITH YOUR NERVES *Dr Tony Lake*	**£2.50**	☐
HOW TO SLEEP BETTER *Dr Peter Tyrer*	**£1.95**	☐
LONELINESS *Dr Tony Lake*	**£1.95**	☐
MEETING PEOPLE IS FUN *Dr Phyllis Shaw* How to overcome shyness	**£1.95**	☐
MID-LIFE CRISIS *Dr Brice Pitt*	**£1.95**	☐
ONE PARENT FAMILIES *Diana Davenport* A practical guide to coping	**£2.95**	☐
SELF-HELP FOR YOUR ARTHRITIS *Edna Pemble*	**£1.95**	☐
SUCCESSFUL SEX *Dr F. E. Kenyon*	**£1.95**	☐
By Dr Paul Hauck		
CALM DOWN How to cope with frustration and anger	**£2.50**	☐
DEPRESSION	**£1.95**	☐
HOW TO BRING UP YOUR CHILD SUCCESSFULLY	**£2.95**	☐
HOW TO DO WHAT YOU WANT TO DO	**£1.95**	☐
HOW TO STAND UP FOR YOURSELF	**£1.95**	☐
JEALOUSY	**£2.50**	☐
MAKING MARRIAGE WORK	**£1.95**	☐
WHY BE AFRAID? How to overcome your fears	**£1.95**	☐

All these books can be ordered direct by post. Just tick the titles you want and fill in the form overleaf.

Name ....

Address ....

....

....

Write to OCP Mail Order, SPCK, Marylebone Road, London NW1 4DU.
Please enclose remittance to the value of the cover price plus:
UK: 50p for the first book plus 30p per copy for each additional book ordered.
Overseas: 75p for the first book plus 45p per copy for each additional book.

Sheldon Press reserve the right to show new retail prices on covers which may differ from those previously advertised in the text or elsewhere. Postage rates are also subject to revision.